## ENDORSEMENTS

Darren Wilson is an extremely important voice in this hour. He is a man of integrity, with an all too rare quality—he is willing to takes risks. I love that willingness because out of that has come wonderful films and books that help disciple a generation in the supernatural lifestyle, naturally. But it's the way he trains that I think is so brilliant: it's through adventure. I have no doubt that this book, *God Adventures*, will once again inspire and train all of us to live the lifestyle that Jesus intended for us. Read and be challenged and changed.

—BILL JOHNSON,
Senior Leader, Bethel Church, Redding, CA

I have great respect for Darren Wilson both as an artist and, more importantly, as a man of God. He chases God the way a songwriter chases a melody, with passion and purpose. He's not afraid to tackle difficult, thorny issues—all because of his desire to know God better and make Jesus famous through everything he creates.

—MICHAEL W. SMITH,
singer and songwriter

Fearless. That's the word that comes to mind when I think of my friend Darren Wilson. Darren has documented so many strange occurrences regarding the supernatural without worrying about his reputation. In his new book *God Adventures*, Darren shares intimate, behind-the-scenes details of some of the most mysterious things God has done in his films. In doing so, he reveals the living Son of God who will stop at nothing to reach the objects of His desire. *God Adventures* has amazing potential to awaken the sleeping non-believer as well as strengthen the faith of the spiritually mature.

—BRIAN "HEAD" WELCH,
Grammy-winning guitarist from Korn and
*New York Times* best-selling author of *Save Me From Myself*

Darren has pushed the boundaries of Christian films to a new level, capturing the heart of the Father in action while at the same time provoking the Body of Christ to take action and trust God to show up. He is an amazing man and a personal friend. I am so thankful for his life and grateful for the gift that he is to the Body of Christ.

—TODD WHITE,
founder of Lifestyle Christianity

I have had the pleasure of knowing Darren Wilson for a few years now and was honored to work with him on a couple of his projects. Whenever I get around Darren, I feel my faith and my hunger to know God rise more. And that is exactly what his new book *God Adventures* will do for you! To hear such incredible stories of the faithfulness and love of Jesus is both inspiring and provoking.

—KIM WALKER-SMITH,
singer and songwriter

I'm going to quote Darren from his own book, *God Adventures*, because I believe it to be important. "God is bigger than our religious bickering about how we minister." In this day and age, it would be a shame to miss this, and this book goes a long way in helping you understand that fact.

—MARC FORD,
singer, songwriter, and former lead guitarist for The Black Crowes

I have personally witnessed Darren Wilson find a deep level of friendship with God through the progression of films that he has produced and my friendship with him. You will find this book a valuable resource for your own spiritual formation. Darren is not just a filmmaker—he is a friend of God.

—CHAD NORRIS,
Senior Pastor, Bridgeway Church, Greenville, SC

*God Adventures* is a true journey on how to see God direct everyday opportunities into becoming miraculous events that reach beyond human ability. Darren Wilson is the real deal and this book is a must read for anyone desiring to encounter the supernatural!

—ROBBY DAWKINS,
minister and evangelist

Step into the world of the supernatural with Darren Wilson's new book, *God Adventures*. A skeptic at first, Darren masterfully takes us on a journey of the undeniable, transforming power of God and how it changed his life. This book could radically alter your walk with God, taking you from the outer court of a boring existence to the holy place of divine encounters. I highly recommend it.

—KRIS VALLOTTON,
Senior Associate Leader, Bethel Church, Redding, CA, and co-founder of Bethel School of Supernatural Ministry

Darren Wilson's honest search to capture the mysteries of God on film has moved many faith mountains for Christians who are just not satisfied with a diluted description of Christ. Darren has a calling to move seeking believers away from the idea that Jesus is "just another historical mythical character," and he allows the Holy Spirit (through his films and ministry) to kick-start them into knowing Jesus as their true and loving God and Savior. Transcribing his experiences and face-to-face meetings with God from the big screen onto paper is the logical next step to expand the legacy of a "normal guy" who wouldn't settle for a man-made god. His tangible experiences will pull you into the miraculous, and his testimony will be a weapon in your arsenal against the enemy.

As Revelation 12:11 says, "And they overcame him by the blood of the Lamb and by the word of their testimony, and they did not love their lives to the death."

—LEON SCHOEMAN,
Director of channels for TBN United Kingdom, Europe, and Africa

# GOD
# ADVENTURES

## Don't Settle for Less
## Than Experiencing More

### DARREN WILSON

**BroadStreet**
PUBLISHING

BroadStreet Publishing Group, LLC
Racine, Wisconsin, USA
www.broadstreetpublishing.com

God Adventures: Don't Settle for Less Than Experiencing More

Copyright © 2016 by Darren Wilson

ISBN-13: 978-1-4245-5269-6
ISBN-13: 978-1-4245-5270-2

Stock or custom editions of BroadStreet Publishing titles may be purchased in bulk for educational, business, ministry, fund-raising, or sales promotional use. For information, please e-mail info@broadstreetpublishing.com.

Edited by Nathanael White
Cover design by Chris Garborg, GarborgDesign.com
Typesetting by Katherine Lloyd, theDESKonline.com

Printed in the United States of America
16 17 18 19 20 5 4 3 2 1

This book is dedicated to my lovely wife, Jenell. If it weren't for you, none of these lessons would have ever been learned, and I'd still be a spiritually dying man. While the world may be a better place because you never gave up on me, my world is a better place simply because you said yes to me. Thank you for being a wonderful wife, a wonderful mother, and a wonderful daughter of the King.

# CONTENTS

one      God Is Mysteriously Good . . . . . . . . . . . . . . . . . . . .11

two      God Is Creative . . . . . . . . . . . . . . . . . . . . . . . . . .27

three     God Is Supernaturally Interactive . . . . . . . . . . . .39

four      God Is the Original . . . . . . . . . . . . . . . . . . . . . . . .55

five      God Is Untaintable . . . . . . . . . . . . . . . . . . . . . . . .67

six       God Is Pure . . . . . . . . . . . . . . . . . . . . . . . . . . . . . 81

seven    God Is the Same to Everyone . . . . . . . . . . . . . . . 91

eight     God Is Gracious . . . . . . . . . . . . . . . . . . . . . . . .103

nine      God Is Focused . . . . . . . . . . . . . . . . . . . . . . . . . 115

ten       God Is Loving-Kindness . . . . . . . . . . . . . . . . . . . 125

eleven    God Is Multicultural . . . . . . . . . . . . . . . . . . . . . .139

twelve    God Is God . . . . . . . . . . . . . . . . . . . . . . . . . . . . .149

Take Your First Step . . . . . . . . . . . . . . . . . . . . . . . . . . . . . . . . . . . . . . 157

Acknowledgments . . . . . . . . . . . . . . . . . . . . . . . . . . . . . . . . . . . . . . 159

About the Author . . . . . . . . . . . . . . . . . . . . . . . . . . . . . . . . . . . . . . .160

# one

# God Is Mysteriously Good

*God isn't limited to doing things we understand; everyone knows that. But does he do things that are patently strange? Would he really cover people in gold dust, drop gemstones at random, and release modern-day manna? Even if he did, why would he do it? The truth is, he does do these things today, strange as it may seem. What's more, these signs and wonders really do show just how good God is.*

When I finished producing my first movie, *Finger of God*, I had no idea how people would react. There had never really been a movie like this, at least nothing about the subject of miracles that had been put together in this way. So I didn't know if I had a strange, quirky movie or something of real power and potency. My honest thought was that I would be lucky if a thousand people saw this film in my lifetime.

But I wanted to make sure I was putting out something that worked on some level, so I gathered around thirty friends, colleagues, and acquaintances into a classroom at Judson University, where I worked, and hit the play button.

Ninety minutes later, the lights came up and I received my

first-ever standing ovation. My sister and brother-in-law came up to me, tears in their eyes, and hugged me. Some people were too emotional to even speak to me. One friend of mine was receiving prayer in the corner, and she was wailing—loudly. At that moment I thought two things:

First, *I think this movie might be on to something*. Second, *Things are never going to be the same again*.

Later that night, I read the comment sheets I had passed out, and boy, for a group of people who had been so overwhelmed by the film, they sure had a lot of specific opinions about it. One opinion stood out above all the others:

"Those first fifteen minutes are going to be a problem."

For those of you who haven't seen *Finger of God*, let me pause and explain what that comment referred to. Basically, in the first fifteen minutes of *Finger of God*, four strange things are shown: 1) people miraculously getting gold teeth, 2) gold dust appearing out of nowhere, 3) manna showing up out of thin air, and 4) gigantic gemstones (as well as little ones) suddenly appearing.

If you've never heard of these things, your first thought is probably, *That's insane*. And if you're a true skeptic, your next thought will be about how you can disprove these claims. The right approach, however, is a balance between cautious discernment and a fertile heart, remembering that God is his own person and can do whatever he likes, whether we're comfortable with it or not. That's at least what I tried to do when I set out to film this stuff.

The only insight I can give on these things is my experience with them. Having made the *Finger of God* movie, I've heard more stories of the supernatural than the average bear. But in the end, I can only speak to what I saw and what happened in front of me. So that's what you're about to read: my eyewitness accounts of these mysterious supernatural acts.

## Gold Teeth

This phenomenon has been happening, as far as I know, since an "outpouring" occurred at the Toronto Airport Christian Fellowship in 1994. Thousands of people have claimed to receive gold teeth, and among those are two people who are very close to me: my Aunt Patsy and Uncle Bob.

Now, the skeptic in me is quite willing to call everyone else claiming this miracle a liar. Indeed, when I filmed John and Carol Arnott, the senior pastors of TACF during the outpouring, John told me they were as interested as anyone in finding out if this was actually happening, and they hired an outside service to come in and investigate the claims as an impartial jury.

What they found was that roughly one-third of the people who claimed God had given them gold teeth had received dental work containing gold in the past and simply forgotten about it amid the hubbub and excitement of the moment. Roughly one-third of the claimants experienced their gold teeth "fading" back to normal teeth for whatever reason. But one-third of the claimants had received no dental work and still had gold teeth shining in their mouths.

I found this information quite helpful. It meant the people in charge were as curious about the truth as I was. It also cemented what I had previously thought—that not every claim of the miraculous was legitimate. Still, I had to contend with one-third of thousands of testimonies.

But even if every other claim had been proven false, I had to face the fact that my aunt and uncle, my own flesh and blood, people I had known my whole life and who were about as normal as you can get (she's a stay-at-home mom; he's a school superintendent), had gone to church one day and left with gold in their mouths. Aunt Patsy got one gold tooth; Uncle Bob got two. This is bizzaro-world to the extreme, and believe me, I was extremely skeptical. But there it was, literally staring me in the face as I looked at my own family.

What people rage against the most with this stuff is not whether it legitimately happens, but that it seemingly serves no purpose. Even if we discount the idea that God might want to do some things just for the fun of it (we do that all the time, and we were created in his image), we are still left with a few explanations. Many people I have talked to who have received gold teeth feel it is a constant reminder that God touched them, that he loves them, and that to him, they are a treasure. It drives them closer into his arms.

Even so, to the outside observer, it seems random, superfluous, and dumb. They say, "There are starving children all over the world, and you're telling me God is going to put gold in someone's mouth? If he's willing to do that, why won't he drop a few hundred dollars into every beggar's hands? Wouldn't that be more helpful?" So we scoff at it and throw it off as lunacy.

Some people say it's the devil trying to trick people with fake signs and wonders, to get their minds off of God and onto this superficial stuff. At first this seems like a good argument. But based on the people I have talked to and on the experience of my aunt and uncle, it doesn't hold water. While it is true that for some observers, the action leads to an unhealthy obsession with chasing after signs and wonders, to the *receiver* it brings a deeper sense of his love for them, and they are humbled, exhilarated, and profoundly affected. I've never met anyone who wants to give it back.

My aunt and uncle went to Toronto in a last-ditch effort to save their marriage (not in pursuit of dental work). Uncle Bob had a tumultuous, abusive upbringing, and as a result became somewhat tumultuous and angry as an adult. Aunt Patsy was commonly referred to as the "super Christian" in our family. Together they obviously had their struggles. Pat wrestled with Bob's anger issues, and Bob grappled with a deep sense of shame and guilt, feeling like a spiritual outcast compared to Pat. His personal issues clouded his sense of self-worth, and that made things worse. By the time they entered the doors in Toronto, it was do-or-die time. God had to show up for them or it was over.

At one point in the service, John Arnott took the stage and announced that he thought God had just released gold teeth in the church, and he told everyone to check their mouths. My aunt and uncle did no such thing. When I talked to them about it afterward, they had very different takes on why they didn't check their mouths, even while those around them did.

Aunt Patsy told me she knew God hadn't done something like that, nor did she particularly care for it, because the whole concept of getting gold teeth was not for her. At least that's what she thought. But later that day, on a lark, their son had her open her mouth so he could check. My cousin Bobby took one look in his mother's mouth and his eyes turned wide with shock. "You got a whopper!" I think was his exact quote.

No one bothered to check Bob's teeth. As he told me, even after his wife got a gold tooth, it never occurred to him that God would do something like that to him because, well, God didn't do those kinds of things to people like him. There was no way God could love him *that* much.

But the next day, when his wife walked beside him to go up to the front of the stage to testify what had just happened to her, my uncle smelled an odor similar to what people smell when a dentist is drilling. As they were leaving the church that night, someone in their party asked Bob to open his mouth so they could check, just in case. They discovered that he had *two* gold teeth. Neither Pat nor Bob knew how to handle it or what it meant, but they were overjoyed that God would touch them in such a strange, unique way.

Shortly after it happened, my aunt received a word during a time of prayer. The word was simple yet powerful: "Pat, I have seen your faithfulness, and I have seen your struggles. I want you to know how proud I am of you, how much I love you. This is, in a sense, your gift for years of loving me despite what it cost you."

Then it was Bob's turn to get a word. "Bob, I want you to realize something very important. You have always felt left out, in a way. You have believed that Pat has earned my love while you have not, and you feel like she is more highly favored in my eyes than you are. But I want you to realize that I gave you a double portion of what I gave to her. I did this not because you deserve it, but because I love you so very much."

Instantly, their hearts melted.

This strange occurrence, which many well-meaning Christians have decried as demonic, was the event that began the restoration of their marriage. They are happily married to this day, and they both have a deeper sense of the Father's love for them, which allows them to love each other more effectively. After all, you can't give love to others if you don't know love yourself.

As far as the legitimacy of the miracle goes, that question has been answered, both in my family and by an independent research firm. And in answer to the accusation that it's demonic, Jesus said that a house divided against itself can't stand (Matthew 12:24–28). The devil isn't in the business of restoring marriages, but God is.

Gold teeth are most certainly straight from God, and they are leading to even more miracles.

## Gold Dust

One of my first personal encounters with gold dust was early on in the filming of *Finger of God*. I went to a meeting in Chicago to try to capture random signs and wonders. At that point in my film career, I didn't have a lot of faith that God would show up and do something for my cameras—but I hoped he would.

I had brought two of my students from Judson to help. When we arrived, I took off my black coat and put it in the corner, on top of one of my students' coats. My other student put his on top of mine. The coat on top of mine was made of cotton sweatshirt material.

The meeting hadn't started yet, and the worship team was practicing. I walked around a bit, set up some cameras, and talked to my guys about what we'd be trying to do that night. At one point, I went back to my coat to get something. When I lifted the sweatshirt off of my coat, I saw that it was coated with gold dust. I called the students over and showed them, and none of us knew what to think about it. I was so shocked that I forgot to film it!

At that meeting, as well as others I attended and filmed, gold dust regularly appeared, usually on people in the audience. Rarely did it fall on the person speaking. I was fascinated by the apparent randomness of where it appeared. Sometimes people freaked out over a fleck of something that sparkled like gold, and everyone crowded around to look at this tiny, microscopic thing. I thought, *This is why people think you all are nuts.* Many people are so hungry for the supernatural that they will grasp at any straw in the hopes that it's the real thing.

This mentality is what turns many people off to these things. There is a common belief that charismatics check their brains at the door when they go to church—and for some people, this is true. But Jesus called us to love him with all our heart, soul, and *mind.* We are to react to what is happening around us with discernment and wisdom, but we must also make certain our hearts are positioned as a child's.

The thought that we must become like children is misunderstood, I think. Hard-core charismatics will tell you that we need to be willing to believe anything. (They actually believe in *every-thing*.) But when my children interact with the world around them, they don't believe everything they see. In fact, I have shown them things that people have sent to me, things that could very well be supernatural, and they have said something like, "It looks like sand to me." They see no need to believe in the supernatural to prove they are right about anything. But they readily believe that if God chooses to do something supernatural, of course it will happen.

Another argument I often hear when people don't want to believe this stuff is that it only happens in America. But since Americans are rich compared to much of the rest of the world, it doesn't make sense that God would give us gold when the streets of Calcutta are filled with starving, homeless men, women, and children. This is proof, they say, that charlatans are behind this.

When I was making *Finger of God*, the idea that millions around the world would see these things I captured and would dissect them in detail was as far from my thinking as the Earth is from the moon. I was just trying to tell a compelling story. I wasn't creating an exposé. I wasn't trying to document hard evidence. Shoot, when Heidi Baker asked me what the movie was about just before I started our interview, my lame answer was "Miracles ... I think." I was just filming the journey of one man (me) who was slowly coming to grips with the infinite possibilities of a limitless God.

Once my film journey left the realm of signs and wonders, I didn't want to return to them or search for them. Of course, I kept hearing of signs and wonders happening everywhere I went—Africa, Eastern Europe, Australia, South America, China. But I was no longer pursuing them as a subject in the movie because the miracles I was encountering were way better and more exciting than shiny objects. But I can understand why people would think that they only happen in America, because that is all I showed.

When I was filming *Furious Love*, my crew and I were walking with some friends on the streets of Jakarta, Indonesia, and a bunch of beggar children approached us for money. We couldn't give them anything without causing a near riot. But we could pray for them, and that's what we did. We laid our hands on their heads and prayed for God's blessing over them, his protection over them, and his provision for them. When we finished, the kids started freaking out because their hands were suddenly covered in gold dust.

When I showed *Finger of God* at Judson University, an American Baptist institution, more than twenty students found gold dust on themselves afterward. Almost none of them had grown up in charismatic circles, and no one knew what to do about this occurrence. None of them screamed that it was from the devil or that someone must have come by and sprinkled it on them without their knowledge. They just worshiped God even more.

Hundreds of people have approached me with stories of their own experiences that seem straight out of a sci-fi movie. These are all normal, wonderful people. They aren't looking for me to put them in my next movie; they just want to talk to someone who will probably believe them. In every case, the act brings them closer to the Father's heart and love for them.

## Manna from Heaven

By the time I was putting my movie together, gold dust and gold teeth were fairly common occurrences. I had heard and seen enough of those things with my own eyes to be confident that much of it was legitimate. But when I encountered manna, that was a whole new ball game.

Manna is tricky for skeptics to disprove because it is in the Bible. The only plausible defense against it is that you don't believe

God is in the business of miracles anymore. That is implausible if you look at the facts.

I knew of only one couple who'd had an experience with manna. Harold and Kaye Beyer, an older couple from Idaho, had apparently seen manna instantly appear, either in Harold's hands or in his Bible, for more than thirty-six years. They kept it secret for a long time because they didn't want people to think they were con artists or insane. When the truth got out, their world turned upside down. This nice, normal Lutheran couple were kicked out of their church, ostracized by their friends, and considered "dangerous."

They came to a church in Chicago to speak, and I showed up with my camera, hoping to capture the manna appearing out of thin air. Hey, a guy can dream, right? By the time the service started, manna had already appeared and I'd missed it. I was pretty bummed about that! But then I found out that it had happened in the hallway just outside the meeting room. Ten people were with Harold and Kaye, some of whom were friends of mine, when suddenly Harold stopped walking and everyone gathered around to pray. All eyes were on this sweet, unassuming eighty-six-year-old man as he put his hands out in front of him. Suddenly, everyone felt a shift in the atmosphere, and instantly his hands were overflowing with manna.

That night, in the service, we had communion … but this time God provided the bread. I didn't film it happening, but more than ten people verified to me that they had seen manna appear with their own eyes. Everyone's story was the same. Either my friends had all conspired to pull the wool over my eyes (what they would gain from that is beyond me), or this supernatural event actually happened. I was convinced this manna thing was real.

Later that year I filmed Canon Andrew White, the vicar of St. George's Church in Baghdad (the only Anglican church in Iraq) and a special envoy to the Middle East appointed by the archbishop of Canterbury. He told me about the time when manna appeared in the hands of some people he worked with closely at the Pentagon.

I now had two separate instances, independent of each other, of God sending manna to people today. It makes me wonder if this phenomenon is common, but because it's so strange, people stay quiet about it.

## Supernatural Gemstones

I'm going to be honest with you: the gemstones thing kind of freaks me out. Even now I have a hard time believing them to be a real occurrence. But as with nearly everything I have encountered, I have been so inundated with normal people telling me their stories and showing me their gemstones that I have to believe at least some of them are telling the truth. I've looked into their eyes and seen the innocent, awestruck wonder they have, even months or years later as they recall the moment when a gemstone appeared out of thin air in front of them.

The gemstones I included in *Finger of God* are large; some are fifty karats. I've been told that some people have taken them to jewelers and gemologists who have said that they don't know what they are. They don't contain the minerals that any other earthly gemstones have. They don't contain microscopic bubbles of man-made material. The experts are baffled by what these things are.

Now, these are things I have been told, so I must take people's word for it. I am hoping to follow up on these claims for a new film series, in no small part because I want to get to the bottom of this issue myself!

I have read reports of people who claimed to have had gems falling in their meetings but were later caught planting gems throughout the sanctuary. Herein lies the difficulty. There are crooks and liars out there. And many people want to believe in the supernatural so badly that they will suspend their own disbelief to accept something as real, despite their better judgment.

Then again, I have talked to many normal, everyday people who have seen gems materialize in the air and then drop in front of them. One said he left his desk at home to grab a Coke and came back to find a gemstone sitting next to his keyboard. Another said she felt a gem hit her foot as she sat listening to someone speak in church. These people have no reason to lie. As a matter of fact, many have a hard time admitting it because they know how unbelievable it is. Those are the people I listen to. Those are the ones I find convincing.

I've personally encountered hundreds of such people. The sheer number of them outweighs my natural, fleshly objections.

## Let Them Decide

Following my film debut of *Finger of God*, as I stared at those sheets of paper in front of me, my heart sank. Everyone who reviewed the movie was warning me that those first fifteen minutes were going to be a problem for a lot of people. Their advice: take it out. The rest of the movie was so fantastic, they said, it didn't need the added weight of these oddities, and I didn't need the added stress. Too many people would turn the movie off after those first fifteen minutes because they would be so skeptical and so offended that they wouldn't give the rest of the movie a chance.

Knowing they were right, I decided to take that section out. But as I was editing the film, I had a conversation with my father. When I told him about my decision to jettison those troublesome first fifteen minutes, he asked me this fateful question: "Son, tell me, do you believe that the things in those first fifteen minutes are from God?"

"Yeah, I think I do," I replied.

"Then you have to include them. It's not up to you to decide what people can or cannot believe. You simply have to show them what you experienced and let them decide. Let the Holy Spirit give them ears to hear. If they reject it, so be it. At least you can say you were obedient."

I knew I had to leave those fifteen minutes in. I also knew I was setting myself up for a major headache.

I don't know why, but for some reason, I seem to have become the patron saint of all things supernaturally wacky. I mean, no one else has made a movie about this stuff. But I struggle with these things just as much as the next guy. I was skeptical about all of the things I heard about when I started making these films, and to some degree I still am.

I have seen people lie. I have seen people stretch the truth. I have seen the naked ambition of some evangelists and pastors. Trust me, if anyone understands the ugly underbelly of belief in the supernatural, it's me. I've seen the problems, the hype, the manipulation. Why then do I still hold fast to the belief that God is in the business of doing strange things today, just as he did in the Bible?

Because the ugly part isn't all I see. For every manipulative evangelist who is pushing people down on stage and making unsubstantiated claims of the miraculous on television, there are a hundred humble, loving individuals around the world quietly doing God's work: loving the unloved and relying on God to show his love to others, often in miraculous ways. They are not asking God to give people gold teeth or drop gemstones in their churches. But when it happens, they do what they are supposed to do: praise God, thank him, and move on to loving the lost.

The real danger of the supernatural is that it can overshadow the natural. We can become so caught up in seeing these things—or attacking or defending these things—that we wind up debating with one another when we should be loving each other.

If you want to call me a heretic, I'll take it, as long as you are loving the person in front of you, even if you disagree with him. I understand that your belief system requires that you try to convince me that what I believe is false. But I think you're wrong too. So we are at an impasse. Either one of us gives, or we continue railing against each other. Or we wise up and realize that there is a dying world all around us, and whether or not Aunt Patsy and Uncle Bob got gold teeth doesn't need to keep us from that dying world.

Look at it this way. I may disagree with my wife about how we should run our finances. It's a real disagreement and it has real consequences. But our different opinions should not lead us to division and hatred. To save our marriage, we need to find a compromise. Above all, we must remain respectful and loving.

The church is a family. But we're squabbling like children while the world looks on.

I have never bought the argument made by some charismatics that questioning these things shows a lack of faith. In 1 Thessalonians 5:21, Paul tells us to "test all things; hold fast what is good" (NKJV). I may test something and find it good. You may test it and find it bad. In the end, we are commanded to "hold firm" to what is good. And that which is most good and most perfect is the love found in Jesus Christ. To that we must hold firm, no matter what.

I have a simple formula for figuring out whether or not I am going to include something in my films. I look at the fruit. Jesus said no good tree can bear bad fruit, just as no bad tree can bear good fruit. If the root of the miracle is bad, it will lead to heartache, pain, and death. If the root of the miracle is God, it will lead to faith, love, and hope. It will lead to restoration, not destruction. It will lead to forgiveness, not bitterness.

If you don't want to believe that Aunt Patsy and Uncle Bob received a touch from God that led to the restoration of their marriage, that is your choice. But don't try to steal their joy away because what happened to them doesn't fit into your own personal experience.

I find it humorous that the people who most often get offended by these miracles teach their children Bible stories in which donkeys talk, iron axe heads float, water pours from rocks, seas part, people are raised from the dead, manna appears out of nowhere for forty years, shadows heal people, men teleport, a woman turns into salt, wooden rods turn into snakes, bushes burn but aren't consumed, the sun stays in one spot for twelve hours, three men stand in a furnace and live, water is turned into wine, food multiplies ... and the list goes on. Compared to that stuff, a little gold dust appearing in a place where the presence of God shows up doesn't seem so outlandish after all—especially when the fruit of it is love.

# two

# God Is Creative

*God's first known act was creation, a work that is filled, by definition, with creativity. And his creativity knows no bounds. As Scripture unfolds, we see him interacting with humankind in ways never before seen. God continues to work today in ways no one has yet experienced, which means that following him requires us to leave our comfortable habits behind to join God in creating a future we have never imagined yet he has always dreamed of.*

If there were ever a poster child for someone surprised by God, it could be me.

Now, I know myself pretty well. But most people only know the part of my history that came after I started making movies about the supernatural. Some people think I'm an expert about these things. They believe I have it all figured out.

Well, I know more than I used to. But the movies I've made are simply the result of God leading me into something new. God seems to avoid people who think they're experts, choosing instead to use people who simply follow him no matter what.

Too many Christians think they're either disqualified or unqualified for what God wants to do through them. They think only "experts" get to do amazing things for God. They don't understand how creative God is, how he can help us face impossible circumstances. And they don't know the intimacy they could have with God if they followed him into something only his creativity can make.

## We Don't Know What God Knows

God taught me a powerful lesson years ago. I had just finished my second movie, *Furious Love*, and had plans to make one more film. At that point, I believed those three films would be it for me. I was going to make a trilogy and be done. But at the premiere for *Furious Love*, God started a process that would show me how powerful his creativity can be.

Because of the later films I made—*Holy Ghost* and *Holy Ghost Reborn*—a lot of people think that I've only made movies based on God's direction and leading. But when I shot those first films, I was still trying to figure things out. Even as I began making my third movie, *Father of Lights*, I was still getting used to hearing the Lord for myself without relying on other people's prophetic words.

At the premiere for *Furious Love*, I sensed that my third movie was going to end in Israel.

At that premiere I met Todd White. I'd heard of him, but I'd never had a strong desire to make a movie with him because I didn't know him.

He said he wanted to meet me. So we hung out for about ten minutes. Honestly, I thought he was a little strange. He kept saying, "I love you, man," which I found weird and awkward. In the middle of that odd conversation, I clearly heard the Lord say, "Ask him to go to Israel with you."

Following the Holy Spirit's prompting, I asked Todd, "Would you consider going to Israel with me to film my next movie?"

He said, "Yeah, that sounds awesome."

I didn't really know this guy. I didn't know what we were going to do in Israel. I just knew that God had told me to go to Israel and to take Todd with me.

## Something Impossible

Before leaving for Israel, I filmed everything else I needed for *Father of Lights*. I was running out of money, but I needed an ending to the movie.

Two days before I left the US, I was in my studio in Chicago having my devotional time. I prayed about my trip to Israel, saying, "Lord, this is the end of my movie-making. We've done a lot of amazing stuff together. But I need you to do something really impressive for this shoot. Would you please allow me to film something totally impossible? Something that no one will be able to say I set up ahead of time, that I somehow made it happen. I want anyone who sees it to say that only God could do that."

I thought maybe God would let me film a resurrection from the dead. That would definitely qualify as something impossible!

When the time for our trip to Israel came, my crew and I met up with Todd on the airplane. I told them what I had prayed. "Keep an eye out. Somebody is probably going to get hit by a car in front of us or something."

For the first two days in Israel, I waited for someone to die so God could raise him from the dead and I could record it on video. It was a really weird feeling.

We filmed some cool stuff during the first three days in Galilee, but none of it was the whiz-bang ending I was looking for.

On our last night in Galilee before traveling to Jerusalem,

we sat in the house of a friend named Gary, who'd been our tour guide. I was looking through a Fodor's tourist guidebook because I didn't know anything about Jerusalem and had never been there.

I came across a picture of the Dome of the Rock and thought, *I've seen this thing before.* The first sentence in the guidebook said, "This is the second holiest site in Islam." The next sentence said, "Since 2001, no non-Muslims have been allowed inside." I asked Gary to tell us about "this dome thingy."

He told me it was the place where Abraham almost sacrificed Isaac, where the ark of the covenant was kept, and where the Holy of Holies was in Solomon's temple.

"That sounds awesome," I said. "We should go up there, somehow get in, and start praying for people. Maybe we can start a revival in the dome!"

Gary laughed. "That's never going to happen. It's impossible."

When I heard that word, I looked at Todd, who was sitting on a couch reading a magazine. Our eyes met, and I could tell we both knew this was a God setup. I turned to Gary and said, "Well, then, that's what we're going to do."

That night we put a prayer request on Facebook, basically telling the world, "Hey, we're asking God for the impossible tomorrow. Start praying for it to happen."

## God's Creative Path

We didn't have any scheduled meetings with anyone when we went to Jerusalem that next day. We had no plan other than to go there and see what God would bring across our path so we could respond to it and follow him.

None of us is an expert at making things happen the way we want them to. But we can invite God to show up and then watch what happens around us. When we step out in risk to follow God's creativity, he works to make the impossible happen through us. People with no experience can simply say yes to God and then follow his leading. In following him, God will lead us into things we know nothing about.

On our way to Jerusalem, we stopped to check out the Jordan River, like any tourists would do. After checking in to the hotel in Jerusalem and freshening up, I said, "Well, I suppose we should probably hit the streets and figure out what we're going to do."

Todd put on a microphone so we could record any conversations he had, then we walked out into the city. Now, in Jerusalem, there are several gates. The Christian gate, for example, leads into the "Christian" section of the city. The crew asked me, "Where do you want to go? Where's the best place to start?"

Since I wanted to get into the dome, I suggested we go to the Muslim gate. When we reached the steps that led to that gate, we found a man in a bright yellow shirt who was limping.

Like a shark smelling blood in the water, Todd practically jumped on the guy, talking to him and asking to pray for him. The rest of us scrambled to turn on the cameras and start filming. Todd politely said, "I know how to take your pain away."

The man seemed intrigued, so Todd asked him to sit with him on a bench. Todd learned that the man had one leg shorter than the other, which threw out his back as he walked. Todd laid hands on the man's legs, and God grew out the short one until they matched. Next Todd laid hands on the man's knee, declaring God's restoration of the discs in his back.

Todd invited the man to stand and see if the pain was gone and the healing was real. He sprung up from the bench, bent over and touched his toes, then lifted his knees and marched along the sidewalk. "Am I dreaming, or what?"

Now, this man was a Muslim. No matter who you are, God

loves you. He will touch you and work miracles in your life whether you believe in him or not.

Obviously I was happy about this miracle. But I wanted to get into the Dome of the Rock! Stopping to pray for one man, even when he got healed, didn't seem to lead us toward the answer to my prayer to see God do something truly impossible, which would give me the ending I wanted for the film.

Still, we all considered this encounter a great start to our day. We spent the rest of that afternoon in the Muslim quarter, mainly in a street market where Todd prayed for people. Soon a small crowd gathered, bringing those who needed healing. All this happened in a part of the city inhabited mostly by Palestinians.

None of this appeared to be moving us toward our goal. But it was certainly where God was leading us.

We had been praying for Muslims for nearly an hour when a man approached us. After he greeted us, Todd asked him if he was healthy. The man said, "No problems. Are you a healing man?"

"Yes, I have this in me," Todd answered.

The man told us to come with him. As he led us out of the market, he asked if we were Christians. After hearing that we were, he told us that he was also a believer and he wanted us to bless his home. One of the roads we followed him down was the Via Dolorosa (which means "the way of Christ's suffering"), one of the streets Jesus walked as he dragged his cross to Calvary.

The man led us to his home, which was just a few blocks from the Muslim market. He introduced us to his father-in-law, who did not speak English. God told Todd that the elder man had problems in his heart and lungs. Our newfound friend confirmed the word, saying his heart was only working 20 percent and was not strong enough to survive surgery.

Todd prayed, and our guide translated. Todd asked the man

how he felt. The man stood and walked around, declaring he was completely healed and had no more pain.

As we were leaving, I asked the son if he knew of any way we could get into the Dome of the Rock. He said it was impossible. I told him I wanted to get in anyway.

He studied me for a long moment. Finally, concluding that we had blessed him, he wanted to bless us. He told us that his best friend knew everyone who worked at the dome, and if there was one person in all Jerusalem who might be able to get us in, it was this man. He asked if we would like to meet him.

Of course we did, so we followed him again. We walked for about twenty minutes through the narrow, winding streets of old Jerusalem. When we came to a courtyard, this man called out to his friend—and it was the man in the yellow shirt whom we had encountered upon entering Jerusalem and watched as God had healed his legs and back!

## "It Was Easy!"

These two friends—a Muslim and a Christian—stood with us in a moment of pure astonishment as God's creativity dawned on each of us. My crew and I had seen no pattern to our steps that day. We'd had no plan. Nothing we'd done had any particular purpose in it except to simply follow God. And even our plan to follow God started with a simple prayer that came from my heart. I'd asked God for something impossible because I wanted to make God famous. Not because I wanted to be famous or sell more movies, but to let God show off. And boy, was he showing off big-time!

We sat with our new Muslim friend and explained what we wanted to do. He told us to come back the next day at ten. The next morning, we met him outside the gate and then made our way to the Dome of the Rock.

Not until I stood outside that ancient building did it really hit me how impossible it was for us to do what we were about to do. This was the place where Abraham almost sacrificed his son Isaac, where the ark of the covenant had been placed inside Solomon's temple, where the blood of sacrifice had been sprinkled once a year on the mercy seat, and where Muslims believed Mohammed ascended into heaven. This was where God tore the veil in two at the moment Jesus died, declaring forever that the separation between God and man had been reconciled.

We were there because we'd followed God, and his creativity found the only plan that could possibly work—one we could not have found on our own. It was all completely and ridiculously impossible.

Yet there we were, following our guide past crowds of tourists taking pictures, through the doors of the dome itself, during the call to prayer. We walked anywhere we wanted completely unhindered, even with cameras and phones.

Our guide asked if we wanted to go into the Well of Souls—the foundation of the Holy of Holies, where God's presence used to reside, where priests could enter only once a year—the one place on earth that had been God's literal, physical home for fifteen hundred years. We went down the stairs into that holiest of places on earth, inviting Jesus to come and be in that place again, releasing his presence. We asked the Holy Spirit to abide in that place as he had done for hundreds of years.

After it was all over, we debriefed with our new friends, the Muslim and the Christian. Our Muslim friend said, his face glowing, "It was easy! God opened the doors for us." No amount of money would have given us access to this place, but God helped us. This was especially surprising because we were Americans.

That's how incredible our creative God is.

## Something Even Deeper

For me, this will always be a special memory because it was the moment that I truly became a friend of God. You see, a friend is someone who trusts you.

This was the first time in my life that my faith outweighed my doubt. After producing three full-length films about God doing surprising, miraculous things, I had finally reached a point where I believed more than I doubted.

God didn't tell me to do this impossible thing. It was my idea. I just asked my heavenly dad, "Will you please do this impossible thing for me so I can show the world how amazing you are?"

I believe that when you come to the Lord with a pure heart that just wants to make Jesus famous, God will move. Because Jesus, God's Son, is his favorite thing.

But God's creativity didn't just accomplish something impossible. He did something personal in me. I saw his heart as I had never seen it before. I felt his love more deeply than I had before. God became more real to me than he had before. I grew more intimate with him through this experience.

Dozens of people received life-changing miracles. A man with a cane threw it aside because his legs were restored. Another man watched his legs grow and received two new discs in his back. Yet another man received healing for a heart that was beyond any surgeon's ability to repair. Two of these men were Muslims. One of them helped us proclaim the testimony of Jesus. The other is best friends with a Christian who can continue helping him see how good Jesus is. Any one of these things could headline a passage of some modern-day book of Acts. But all of these happened as paving stones on the path to an impossible prayer, which God answered to reveal how good he is and how much he loves me.

God didn't just get me into the Dome of the Rock. He led me

down an incredible string of impossible miracles just to get my foot in the door. He didn't have to do any of those things, but he did. Because he loves me. And because he loves his Son, Jesus.

And he loves you too.

By nature, God is both supernatural and creative. Because he is creative, he is always doing something new, making things that didn't exist before. And because he is supernatural, the things he does will always be things that are impossible for us humans.

If you put those two attributes together, you come up with a recipe for risk. You can't join God in his supernatural creativity without walking toward things that only exist in your imagination once God speaks to you about them. Hebrews 11:3 says, "By faith we understand that the worlds were prepared by the word of God, so that what is seen was not made out of things which are visible" (NASB). The chapter goes on to list story after story of people who believed God for things that were invisible, but their faith in him helped make them visible.

Noah had never seen rain, but he believed God enough to spend a hundred years building a boat. As a result, he was saved when God flooded the earth. Abraham and Sarah physically couldn't have children, but Abraham believed God for descendants he would never see. Joshua couldn't see the force that would destroy Jericho's walls, but he faithfully marched around the city, believing an invisible God was stronger than a visible fortress.

Walking supernaturally with a creative God means we will have to reach into an invisible world that only exists in God. And with God, to pull that world into ours so that what was impossible becomes real right before our eyes. There's nothing special about people who do that, except that God chose them. He's the one who qualifies us. All we have to do is be childlike enough to believe what he says about us, step out, and take the risk for the sake of making Jesus famous.

That is what happened in Jerusalem. I was out of money, out of time, and out of options. Yet I believed this was the direction God wanted me to go. While God was making the way for it to happen, I rejoiced in what looked like a string of miracles—wonderful in themselves, but not what I'd asked for or needed. The invisible thing I had prayed for in faith didn't become real until God connected the dots in that courtyard.

Every step was a step into the invisible. Each step of faith led us to the dome.

What steps has God been talking to you about lately? What invisible thing has he put into your heart, asking you to partner with him through faith to make it become real in the world today? What community near you pursues this God of faith to grab hold of impossible things? How can you spend time there and learn to live as they do? Or how can you start that kind of community?

There are no experts. There are only people who say yes to God to take risks for him. Will you say yes to him today?

three

# God Is Supernaturally Interactive

*The supernatural is real. It affects us every day. But many people, Christians included, discount the power and reality of the spiritual realm because they haven't experienced it for themselves. The stories recorded here show just how real the spiritual world is—both light and dark—and how we can safely embrace this truth in our everyday lives.*

I didn't grow up believing the supernatural was real. In fact, quite the opposite. I was skeptical, and still am to this day.

But if something is true, I'm on the hook for it, whether I like it or not. That's how my journey to make *Finger of God* began. By the end of that journey, I had seen and filmed so many miraculous happenings that even my skeptical mind was convinced they were real.

As much as that altered my life, I didn't expect anything more to come of it. I had no plans to make more movies. I was a college professor and happy to stay that way. But those plans changed when I felt God asking me to make another movie, called *Furious Love*. It was going to be about spiritual warfare, and it was going to be a lot more intense than *Finger of God*.

Jeff Jansen, an evangelist, asked me to come with him to Tanzania to film a crusade he was doing there. It sounded pretty simple, so I agreed. I figured I would film some crowd scenes where everyone goes wild for God. We'd capture a ton of salvations, which would be great stuff for that new film.

That just goes to show how little I understood anything.

At that film shoot I saw a lot more happening in the spiritual world than I'd ever seen. It all began in an unassuming white tent set up off to the side of the main tent. I figured it must be for the hearing impaired. That's where everything I'd known about the spiritual world would be destroyed.

The crusade started with singing, dancing, and preaching, followed by an altar call. Everything seemed perfectly normal. But when Jeff prayed, the crusade became a war zone. Men and women began screaming, falling down, and convulsing. Teams of prayer ministers raced to those on the ground and carried them away, practically dragging them kicking and screaming off to the side.

That's when I realized the little white tent wasn't for the hearing impaired. It was the demon tent.

## Abercrombie Girl

I never expected anything like this to happen. As I scrambled in the chaos, not just for a good shot but to understand what was happening, one girl stood out to me. She was wearing an Abercrombie sweatshirt. She came forward for the altar call, and after Jeff prayed his prayer, she started to manifest a demon.

A couple of men whisked her away to the demon tent, and I followed. All the men and women who had begun convulsing throughout the large field when Jeff prayed were now crammed into this one small tent, and they were still shaking, flailing, and flopping on the ground. Ministry teams worked to restrain them to keep them from hurting themselves and others. Everyone was shouting. Ministry workers were shouting to get the demons out, and demonized people were screaming because they were demonized.

Abercrombie girl was screaming too. I never thought I'd be face-to-face with a demon-possessed person. It was horrible enough just watching, but it was worse when I had someone translate what she was saying.

"I'm not coming out!" she screamed over and over. This went on for so long, I finally had to step outside to get some fresh air.

God had already broken himself out of many of my boxes with the miracles, healings, gold teeth, gemstones, and manna I'd witnessed when making my earlier films. But after that, I thought I could go back to my normal, comfortable, Western church life. I mean, what else was there to film? But the reality I discovered in Tanzania was startling. This was my first exposure to the great war of the invisible.

My skeptical mind quickly skimmed through all the potential explanations for what I had seen. Maybe all these people were crazy. But could all these people behave normally until the name of Jesus was invoked over their lives, then all of a sudden have insanity show up in all of them at the same time? I don't think so.

Maybe they'd all been planted there to make a more dramatic show. But planted by whom? How would Jeff benefit from this if it were an act? It made his events messy, which made for more work, more volunteers needed, more training beforehand. And it would cost money, not make money. No, this wasn't some coordinated, planned act.

If these people weren't insane, and they weren't hired performers, there was only one logical conclusion. They'd been caught in the middle of something much bigger than themselves.

What do we do if we've grown up in a world where this sort of scene is reserved for science fiction or horror movies? How do we respond? Do we ignore all logic and deny it? Or do we open ourselves to the possibility that there is much more to our world than what we have seen before?

I can't deny what I saw that day. When I went into that little white tent, I discovered a world that was bigger than I'd known before.

Having survived the destruction of my own little Christian bubble, I want to help you walk through the same process.

## Where Your World Comes From

In the beginning, God created the world. But it's remarkable how different one person's view of the world is from that of others.

Anthropologists—the people who study humans and human culture around the world—call this our worldview. Simply put, a worldview is how someone defines what is real.

When you travel the nations of the world, you'll find a schism between the East and the West when it comes to what people believe to be real. In general, the East believes in the supernatural world; the West doesn't. Architects in the East design buildings with spiritual principles in mind, from ancient pagodas to modern high-rises. In the West, buildings are designed with practicality and utility in mind. Eastern people practice rituals for luck, for blessings, or to appease the spirits. Westerners tend to think that's all superstition.

We all think we understand what the world is really like. Maybe we don't consciously think that, but the way we live our lives is built on the assumption that we have a grasp on reality. After all, it's hard to go through life if we question what is real.

This is tricky, though, because if we want to understand what the world is actually like, we have to look at the whole world, not just our little corner of it. We need to take in the experiences of people who are different from us. We must realize that another person's experiences can be valid and true, even if they are far different from anything we've experienced.

Of course, when people talk about weird supernatural things, we have to wonder if they're just making it all up. But what would anyone gain by faking being possessed by a demon? Why would people endanger themselves by throwing themselves violently to the ground? It doesn't make sense.

I spent my life not wanting to know too much because knowledge meant responsibility. But once I saw for myself that there was something beyond me, that I was in the middle of a spiritual war whether I wanted to be or not, I had to know more.

So get ready, because I'm about to prove to you that Abercrombie girl and that little white tent were not just isolated incidents. The supernatural realm is constantly at work around us, all over the world. And a lot of it is really, really dark.

## The Mystic Banquet

I once interviewed a man named George Otis Jr. He's the creator of the popular video series *Transformations,* and he has spent decades traveling the world, researching and documenting the spiritual realm.

He told me about a ritual from Tibetan Buddhism called *chuud,* which means "the mystic banquet." In their belief system, this ritual is supposed to be a shortcut to enlightenment—the "heaven" all Buddhists live for. A Buddhist believes that people normally have to go through countless life cycles of reincarnation, building karma in each life cycle, until they finally escape the cycle into enlightenment. This enlightenment is basically seen as the end of existence, or the reabsorption into some sort of universal consciousness where one loses all sense of self. The *chuud* ritual is supposed to allow you to skip over all the cycles of reincarnation. But because you could die in the process, only the most radical people try it.

George told me these radicals will live alone in a cave for years so they can practice the visualization techniques they'll need for the final ritual. They do this until they can visualize themselves cutting off the top of their skull and removing it so it becomes a bowl. That's when they leave their cave and go somewhere they know demons gather. Once there, they play an instrument made from a hollow human thighbone. Using this instrument and a drum, they call hundreds of demons to come for the "mystic banquet." They will spend hours performing this ritual process.

Once they visualize taking off their skull cap, they will continue dismembering their entire bodies, piece by piece, putting it all in the skull cap until there is nothing left of them. Finally, they'll play their music again, inviting all these demons to come and feast. The feast is everything they put into their skull bowl, their entire personhood and existence.

George concluded ominously, "And these demons do come."

This isn't a fictional scene from some Hollywood movie. This is anthropological research done by a real person. And this is not research about past history, but about something that is happening now. Thousands of living people have attempted it in Tibet, Bhutan, and Nepal.

George traveled to Bhutan with some colleagues, and they climbed a mountain in the dark to a remote temple so he could interview a man who, by Buddhist measures, had successfully completed this ritual. As they rose higher into the mountain toward this temple, the darkness became so thick it was palpable. When they walked down the final hallway to where George would interview the priest, it felt as if they were being physically touched by invisible spirits that surrounded them.

This is the testimony of a modern-day scientist! But what George described to me was gruesome.

When these radicals invite demons to the feast, a large number of them go insane or die. Because when all these demons come to the banquet, it's not visualization anymore. They really do come and consume these people, just as they were invited to do.

George said his research led him to incredibly graphic reports by secular anthropologists and ethnologists who have witnessed these rituals. Mostly unbelievers, they have watched demons manifest to consume a human being. And they describe it as the most terrifying moment of their lives.

Unbelievers are writing scholarly papers about supernatural encounters. But what if you found out such things were going on right in your own backyard?

## The Fifth Bride of Satan

One day a woman named Angela Greenig came to my studio in Chicago to introduce me to a girl she had helped lead out of satanism. For her safety and protection, we'll call this girl Esther.

When I sat down with Esther, she told me a prominent satanist had prophesied before she was born that one of the brides of Satan would fall and would therefore need to be replaced. He named a hospital, date, and time, declaring that a girl would be born then and there who would replace the fallen bride. Esther was that baby.

The satanists took her and raised her. She was trained her entire life for one purpose—to marry the devil.

Greenig didn't understand what she was about to get herself into when she agreed to meet with Esther. She had done hundreds of deliverances and was told that Esther was high up. But she didn't realize just how high.

Greenig remembers the day they met. When Esther was a few

blocks away, the darkness became so intense that the ground shook. When Esther arrived, she opened the car door without touching the door with her hands, just her demonic powers. Her eyes were pitch black—no white was visible in them at all.

Catching the car door as Esther flung it open, Greenig said, "I don't think so, babe." It was the first time in Esther's life that anyone had challenged her. The demons inside Esther responded immediately, turning Esther's head in three directions and shooting back at each angle, "We know who you are! We know who you are! We know who you are!"

Greenig wasn't about to allow the demons to engage in a real fight. She asked Esther, "Do you want Jesus or Satan? Which will it be?" A little girl rose out of that demonized woman just long enough to gasp, "Help me!" before the demons pulled her back.

This isn't your normal "girl next door," but it all happened, right there near one of America's biggest cities—more evidence that the spiritual world is real, just as real as our natural world.

After about twenty minutes with Angela, Esther was delivered and set free. But while she's given her life to Jesus, her earthly story still has trials.

Angela and Esther have dealt with attempted kidnappings and other efforts from satanists to get Esther back. One time the women found an infant's severed pinky surrounded by a ring of stones right outside her front door—evidence of a satanic ritual. A clear message that the darkness was real and it hadn't forgotten.

## Shanti

By now you're getting the message loud and clear that there is more to our world than is often acknowledged in our Western culture. But I want to tell you about one more person whose story will help peel back the veil even more completely. I'll call her Shanti, again to keep her safe, as she is continually in danger of persecution.

Shanti lives in India and travels all over the world, spreading the good news of Jesus to the poor. She has a school and is creating a home for children from the lowest caste in India: the untouchables.

Let me set some context. Everything in India is spiritual. Even their traditional greeting, *namaste*, literally means "to the god in you." India's primary religion, Hinduism, is the reason for the nation's caste system, a thriving culture of oppression built off their idea of karma. They believe those born in low castes did terrible things in a previous life, so they treat low castes viciously to punish them for a history no one actually remembers but everyone assumes is real.

India is one of the few nations in the world with a rising disparity between the birthrates of boys and girls. They intentionally abort female fetuses and kill infant girls at such a high rate that it shows in their population statistics.

All of this happens in a nation where buildings are shaped in the images of demons, where the demonic is feared, worshiped, and celebrated.

I witnessed this firsthand when I traveled to India to meet Shanti and went to the temple of Kali, the Hindu goddess of death and destruction. A family had come to the temple and was performing a ritual. They took hair from their baby's head, put it into some dough, and offered that up to their god as thanks for its help in conceiving the child.

Elsewhere in the temple, a family sacrificed a goat. They prayed to the goat, then chopped off its head and anointed the entire family, kids included, with its blood.

As I watched parents ritually presenting their children to the goddess of death and destruction, I remembered the Buddhist priests and their ritual. I don't even want to imagine the evil that was being invited into those families.

But I didn't go to India to visit Hindu temples. I was there to hear about something horrendous that was taking place in the Indian countryside of Orissa. Hindu extremists had massacred thousands of Indian Christians in recent years, and the news media was all but ignoring it.

Shanti organized a meeting where survivors of this persecution could come together in hopes of finding some solace and healing through their common bond, Jesus. Our attempt to attend the meeting ended when a train in front of us derailed, nearly killing us all. We had left a camera with Shanti and were forced to smuggle it out later. What we found on the tape was shocking.

In 2008, a steady wave of persecution rose for four straight months until it reached its peak, but then it didn't stop. It just kept going. No one intervened because no one knew it was happening. All the media was kept out.

The persecution systematically destroyed Christians by burning each village church first, so that when they started burning homes, the Christians would have no place to hide. When families realized there was no safety at the church, they ran, often splitting up. Husbands would run one way while the wives and children sought shelter in the jungle. But the next day, they couldn't find each other again. Often days later, they found out that their husbands, wives, and children had been killed.

This happened throughout an entire region of India. To grasp the scope of this, imagine that terrorists were systematically going from city to city throughout New York, burning churches and homes while slaughtering the families who lived there. Imagine this going on for month after month and no one coming to help.

GOD IS SUPERNATURALLY INTERACTIVE


This is the evil Shanti confronted by comforting the believers left homeless and broken.

We may see this massacre as the work of some deranged madman, someone whose head isn't working right. But this isn't an isolated problem, and there is no singular leader running the operation. It is a cultural movement inspired by demons. It is a supernatural effort to quench anything that would threaten the control of a demon of death and destruction.

## How God Sees the World

This supernatural world I've described is what the majority of the world knows to be real. But what is God's worldview?

In the Bible, every page is supernatural. Some stories describe supernatural events—creation, the flood, God's encounters with Abraham, the ten plagues, and so on, all the way to John on the island of Patmos receiving the great Revelation. Other passages record the declared word of God to his people, as in the books of the prophets. Every single one of these encounters testifies of a supernatural realm that is constantly interacting with the natural one.

Every time God speaks, it's supernatural. Every time he does something, it's supernatural. When he created angels (some of whom became demons through rebellion), he created a supernatural realm that is outside our natural ability to see or hear.

Jesus came as the ultimate union of natural and supernatural, violating all boundaries between the two. He had one message: "The kingdom of heaven is at hand" (Matthew 4:17 NASB).

Now, when I sit at my desk, I make sure my coffee is "at hand." In other words, it's within my reach, not far away. The Western way of thinking looks at anything supernatural as either nonexistent or so far off that we can't reach it. Jesus' incarnation shows this can't be true—it combined the natural and supernatural in one human body.

Every believer in Jesus gets to experience this reality for himself! After Jesus rose from the dead, he gave the Holy Spirit to the disciples, then to all who believed, and then to all the converts they made. Paul described this by saying, "Do you not know that you are God's temple and that God's Spirit dwells in you?" (1 Corinthians 3:16 NRSV). You cannot be a Christian without becoming a living union between the natural and the supernatural!

So why should we be surprised if the supernatural realm sometimes shows itself? Why should we be surprised if angels and demons are real, if light and darkness are actual influences over people all over the world, including us?

After all, the apostle Peter said, "Be sober-minded; be watchful. Your adversary the devil prowls around like a roaring lion, seeking someone to devour" (1 Peter 5:8). And the apostle Paul said, "For we do not wrestle against flesh and blood, but against the rulers, against the authorities, against the cosmic powers over this present darkness, against the spiritual forces of evil in the heavenly places" (Ephesians 6:12). If this truth was real enough for Peter and Paul to warn us about it, who are we to think it somehow stopped being true?

## Your Foundation of Reality

We could go through the Bible and find all the passages that show the reality of a supernatural realm that daily interacts with our normal, natural world. But when it comes down to it, you have to experience it for yourself.

The reason you and I and those people on the other side of the world define reality so differently is that we all define it based on what we have experienced. Worldview *defines* what we believe to be real, but our experiences *build* what we believe is real.

If you grew up in a normal Western home, avoiding interaction with the supernatural and instead learning a scientific, naturalistic way of interpreting the world around you, your experiences will have led you to believe a "reality" that excludes the supernatural.

But let's say you grew up in a charismatic Christian home and you've seen God heal people, or you have given prophetic words to strangers with knowledge about them only God could give you. Then your worldview would make room for the supernatural.

On the darker side, drug use often leads people into supernatural experiences, and so can sexual abuse. Even common children's games like Ouija boards or table levitation have given thousands of people supernatural experiences that have shaped what they believe is real.

If you struggle to believe the supernatural is real today, think back on the environment you grew up in. Did it shelter you from possible supernatural experiences? Did it shape you in a way that leads you to doubt the supernatural?

Or did you struggle with the stories I shared here because they all focus on darkness instead of light? All Christians believe in God, and most believe in supernatural forces of light, but many have a hard time believing in the demonic. Everything evil in the world is boiled down to fallen human nature and psychological disorders. They don't believe in any influence beyond this, certainly not in their own lives.

But the stories I've written about are real. God is real, angels are real, and demons are real. They are all active in the world around us today. And we can interact with them … for better or for worse.

## Spreading God's Reality

This final story, like the others I've shared, demonstrates the reality of the supernatural. But unlike the others, this one shows the power of light to give someone a new reality.

Esther told me this story the day she came to my studio. For much of her life, she had been able to see angels and demons. She saw angels as beings shining with light. Her family of witches told her to stay away from anyone light because that person might try to lead her away from the coven.

One day two satanists took her to curse Benny Hinn—a well-known signs-and-wonders evangelist—at one of his stadium crusades. When she saw him, she saw a powerfully bright light shining around him and felt a deeply charged atmosphere. She saw light throughout the whole stadium.

She was afraid of the light, assuming Hinn was a white wizard, the kind of person she'd been taught never to mess with because she could die. The witches with her assured her they would all be okay, but Esther still said they should hurry up and curse Hinn so they could get out of there.

Esther had a feeling something was going to happen. She wasn't disappointed. After a time of worship, Hinn got up to speak. In the middle of his sermon, he stopped suddenly and pointed up to the nosebleed seats where Esther and her two witch friends were sitting. "You three devil worshipers, stop cursing me. I'm a child of God."

Esther knew they were in trouble and tried again to get her companions to take her out of there. But before they could leave, Hinn gave Esther and her friends a direct prophetic word. "I want you guys to know that if you don't give your souls to Jesus, Satan will drag your souls to hell. And I see one of you, you're going to get saved soon. So everybody, all you believers in Jesus, stretch your hands over toward that section and start praying."

Immediately Esther felt like electricity was going through her body, and she screamed. The power of the saints' prayers was so strong that she went in and out of consciousness. The whole room filled with light, full of angels. The light went everywhere, and Esther knew it was the presence of God.

A few weeks after the crusade, Esther met Angela, got delivered, and was saved by Jesus.

Esther's story shows us that light and darkness isn't just a metaphor for good and evil. They're real. When Jesus said, "You are the light of the world. … Let your light shine before others, so that they may see your good works and give glory to your Father who is in heaven" (Matthew 5:14–16), he was talking about something real. It may not be physically tangible, but it is spiritually tangible, and it makes a difference in the world around us.

Jesus wasn't just speaking figuratively. We really are the light of the world, and when God's light shines in the darkness through us, the darkness cannot overcome it (John 1:5). Esther's life was transformed because people shined their light on her darkness and overcame it.

This means two things. First, it means that our worldview—what we believe is real—has to be settled. The supernatural is real. It's everywhere.

Second, what matters most is that Jesus sent us to shine our light on those around us, regardless of what they believe, until they see God's reality, turn to him, and let him turn their darkness to light.

# four

# God Is
# the Original

*The very existence of demonic power is proof of God's power, because Satan doesn't create anything. He only perverts what God creates. We cannot reject all spiritual power, assuming it's all demonic. Instead, we need to learn how to tell the difference between God's power and the power of demons. Once we learn this lesson, the church can become powerful, united, and free.*

You're probably thinking, *This guy's crazy!*" Believe me, you're not the first. I've heard that a lot.

But why is what I believe crazy? Why shouldn't we expect the world to be exactly like the stories I've told? We see those same kinds of stories in the Bible. Did God change? Did demons go away or forget how to be overtly powerful?

I don't think so. Which means something else is going on.

In these next few pages, I'll give you the best explanation I have. I'll also show you one of the tools I use as I sort through thousands of spiritual stories to figure out what's real, what's fake, what's demonic, and what's genuinely God.

## Counterfeit Spirits

Some people say that my friends and I operate in a "counterfeit spirit." Which means that all the supernatural stuff I show in my movies is done with demonic power. They say this because they reason, "God doesn't work that way."

This argument reached a whole new level after my fourth movie, *Holy Ghost*. That is the most controversial film I have made yet. But I was not prepared for the backlash against it. I mean, there was no neutral with that movie. People either loved it or hated it.

Now, I expected there to be some negative response to how I featured the heavy-metal band Korn in the movie. But what surprised me was how strongly people reacted to my trip to Salt Lake City with Jamie Galloway and Will Hart. That trip earned us a lot of "false prophet" and "counterfeit spirit" talk, particularly because of how Jamie and Will ministered while we were there.

One of the first things the Lord told me when I started praying about *Holy Ghost* was to go to the Mormon temple in Salt Lake City and pray for Mormons. At the time, I didn't know much about Mormons. I'd heard they were pseudo-Christians or something like that, but that was it. I did some research before we went, and when we got there and started hanging out with former Mormons, I learned that their version of Jesus is quite different from the biblical Jesus. They don't even believe he's God. They say he's a created being, the brother of Lucifer.

For the sake of my film, I was more interested in what Mormons believe about the Holy Spirit. I discovered that they believe in a Holy Spirit, but they wouldn't say anyone interacts with the Holy Spirit. To them, the Holy Spirit is pretty much the idea of providence, or some concept of God distantly guiding world events, not an actual person you can encounter.

That became our focus as we dove into the heart of Mormon country. Everyone there believed in holiness, and we didn't have to convince them the Holy Spirit is real. We just needed to show them he's an actual person who can be encountered.

That's what Jamie and Will focused on in the film. Our message was, "We're going to give you an encounter with the Holy Spirit because he's in love with you and he wants a relationship with you."

Now, for Christians, there is nothing controversial about that. This has been the gospel message for two thousand years. It's hard to imagine how we attracted so much criticism from fellow believers. But we did, because of how we presented this message.

We went around town near the Mormon temple, and Jamie and Will prayed for people on the streets. Jamie or Will would approach someone and say, "Hey, I want to show you something." If the person was willing to give us some time, they asked the person to hold out his hands as if he were going to receive a present.

Then Jamie or Will held their hands out over the stranger's outstretched hands and prayed, "Holy Spirit, come." They waited a few seconds, then asked if the person felt anything. Almost every time, people experienced some sort of physical sensation. Some felt unexplainable heat, some felt as if electricity were coursing through them. Some felt a weightiness rest on them like a blanket or a sense of peace filling their hearts.

Whenever the person they prayed for felt something, Jamie or Will prayed, "Double it." This was the beginning of trouble for me.

## Accusation and Answer

Negative messages poured in through online message boards, direct correspondence, and even protests outside some of our movie events. People all over the country took offense to the ministry we did in Salt Lake City because of how Jamie and Will prayed. They felt it was disrespectful, acting like we could command Holy Spirit to do things, as though he were a circus monkey or we were doing a magic show. They all used the same verse to back up their claim that we had a counterfeit spirit: 1 John 4:1, which says, "Beloved, do not believe every spirit, but test the spirits to see whether they are from God, for many false prophets have gone out into the world." The implication was that they had tested our spirits and found us to be false prophets. Don't ask me when or how they conducted this test, because I'd never met these people in person. They'd never talked with me, never asked about my testimony.

These people apparently didn't read the next verses, which say, "By this you know the Spirit of God: every spirit that confesses that Jesus Christ has come in the flesh is from God, and every spirit that does not confess Jesus is not from God" (1 John 4:2–3). The apostle John wrote these verses to address a specific situation at a specific point in history—the rise and threat of Gnosticism in the church. These verses define the test John spoke of in the first verse.

Apparently, these accusers hadn't watched my movies to see whether they confessed Jesus, because they do at every turn.

Other accusers used a different verse to make essentially the same point, quoting, "For false Christs and false prophets will arise and perform great signs and wonders, so as to lead astray, if possible, even the elect" (Matthew 24:24). The assumption is that my films feature false signs and wonders intended to "lead astray, if possible, even the elect."

If it were easy to spot false Christs and false prophets, they would never deceive anyone! If all signs and wonders were false, Jesus wouldn't have needed to warn us against them. Or his warning would have simply said, "If you see anyone besides me using supernatural power, don't believe them!"

Instead, Jesus told us, "Truly, truly, I say to you, whoever

GOD IS THE ORIGINAL

believes in me will also do the works that I do; and greater works than these will he do, because I am going to the Father" (John 14:12). Jesus' works were an incredible variety of every kind of miracle imaginable, so this promise is pretty amazing. Jesus did not make this promise only for the apostles sitting around the table with him at the Last Supper, but also to "whoever believes" in him, including you and me.

Our baseline for living is the example Jesus set for us, and our goal is to do even more signs and wonders than he did. So it seems impossible for the presence of signs and wonders to be proof of demonic power in and of itself.

For signs and wonders to qualify as *false*, there have to be *genuine* signs and wonders as well. You can't have counterfeit thousand-dollar bills because there aren't genuine thousand-dollar bills. The devil can't fake something God isn't doing, so you can't say that just because someone performs signs and wonders they do them with the power of a "counterfeit spirit."

Sometimes my accusers try this one: "Even Satan disguises himself as an angel of light. So it is no surprise if his servants, also, disguise themselves as servants of righteousness" (2 Corinthians 11:14–15). I'm not sure what they mean by this, because they don't say anything else to help me understand why they think I'm disguising darkness in a lie of light.

The problem Paul was talking about had to do with certain people who discovered they could get money and fame by posing as apostles and traveling from church to church. The Corinthians had been taken in by at least one of these people, leaving Paul in the awkward place of needing to defend his genuine apostleship— not for his own sake, but for the sake of those he shepherded. If he lost his influence among them, he would lose his ability to serve and help them. In the context of this verse, his defense was that he never asked the Corinthians to support him financially, but instead burdened churches from other cities so he could give himself to them freely.

Paul addressed the issue of money grabbing and fame seeking, not an issue of signs and wonders. The complaint against me, however, seems to be that I promote a powerful God who does signs and wonders. And in the case of Jamie and Will, that they went too far.

## Judge the Fruit

There's one more passage that gets thrown at me frequently, and it really gets to the heart of situations like Jamie and Will's. Ironically, it's the one I find best helps us discern what is God at work and what is not.

This passage is Matthew 7:15–16, which says, "Beware of false prophets, who come to you in sheep's clothing but inwardly are ravenous wolves. You will recognize them by their fruits. Are grapes gathered from thornbushes, or figs from thistles?" This warning often gets lumped together with the others I talked about in the previous section. Most of these warnings include clear instructions for how to know when to heed the warning and when not to, as this one does.

Jesus said that we can know a tree by its fruit. We are easily able to discern good fruit from bad fruit in agriculture, and Jesus says it should be just as easy for us to discern false prophets from true servants of God because we know them the same way.

There was a time in Jesus' ministry when he needed to point to his own fruit to defend himself from those who accused him of operating in a counterfeit spirit. We find that story in Matthew 12:22–37, which I'll summarize here.

A demon-oppressed man was brought to Jesus, and Jesus set him free. The result of his freedom was also his healing so that he could see and speak. People started clamoring about whether Jesus might be the Messiah, so the religious leaders tried to dissuade them by saying, "It is only by Beelzebul, the prince of demons, that this man casts out demons" (12:24).

Jesus responded by saying that a kingdom divided against itself cannot stand. He showed how nonsensical it was to think Satan would be casting out Satan, because then he would be defeating himself. If Jesus was casting out demons and healing people, it had to be the work of God done by the Spirit of God through a servant of God—nothing counterfeit about it.

In the final verses of this passage, Jesus repeated his teaching that we know a tree by its fruit.

If a miracle brings freedom, healing, restoration, redemption, and wholeness, it is a work of God. If it brings bondage, destruction, oppression, sickness, loss, or death, it is a work of Satan. If it leads to people praising God, if it connects people more deeply to him, or if it reveals God's heart, it is probably a work of God. But if it separates people from God or leads to their independence from him, it is probably a work of Satan.

Don't look at the work by itself; look at what it produces. Jesus once spat in a blind man's eyes, but that's what gave him sight. He called a woman a dog and told her he wouldn't heal her child, only to change his mind because of her earnest faith. Another time he delayed visiting a dear friend who was sick because he knew God's plan was to raise him from the dead and he hadn't died yet. I wonder how it would have gone over if Jamie or Will had done any of those things on the streets of Salt Lake City.

## What If It Was You?

When Jamie, Will, and my film crew came with me to the streets of Salt Lake City, the whole point was to lead people to encounter the Holy Spirit deeply and personally. As person after person unmistakably felt the Holy Spirit touching them, and my friends prayed, "Double it," that wasn't a command. They weren't bossing God around. What they did might comes across a little show-man-like, but these guys are two of my best friends. They are the sweetest, most humble guys in the world.

Now, to be honest, I was pushed a little outside my comfort zone by what we were doing there, so I asked Jamie, "Is that how you would normally minister to people?"

"No," he said. "I just really felt the Lord telling me to do some of these things."

How can I argue with that? I mean, here's a guy I know and trust. I've seen him minister before. I know the fruit of his ministry. I know his heart. And there on the streets of the city, I saw the fruit of his prayers time after time. There was no denying that people were encountering the Holy Spirit. They felt his power going through their bodies, and they left the encounters closer to God because of it.

As Jamie and Will prayed for people, they received prophetic words for them and words of knowledge about things that needed to be healed. If you're unfamiliar with prophetic words, let me explain that it's nothing like the judgmental prophesies of the Old Testament. Like everything else in our lives, Jesus' work on the cross changed prophecy so that now a prophetic word is all about the amazing things God has in store for someone, calling out the "gold" inside them, and encouraging them. When Will and Jamie prophesied over people, they were strengthened and comforted, emboldened to walk with God into all he desires for them.

The words of knowledge Will and Jamie received opened opportunities to pray for people to get healed, and they were healed. It's hard to get upset about broken people being fixed. I mean, imagine yourself walking down the street with pain in your

GOD IS THE ORIGINAL

body, and a couple of random strangers stop you and invite you into a heavenly encounter. Before you know it, anxiety is washing off your mind as you become filled with God's peace. Whatever weighed on you before is now being replaced by joy simply because a stranger said, "Holy Spirit, come."

The stranger asks how you're feeling, and you tell him. He says, "Double it." Who wouldn't want double the joy and peace you're feeling now?

Then these two men tell you things you've never told anyone, the deepest hopes of your heart. You know it's God talking to you through these men. More than ever, you know God is real, that he knows you and loves you.

One of these strangers asks if you have pain. He mentions the exact place in your body that's been troubling you. They pray. The pain leaves your body. You're healed!

Finally, these two men ask if you know Jesus. Yes, you say, but not like these men have shown him to you. They offer to introduce you to this amazing Jesus Christ and his Holy Spirit. After what you just experienced, there's nothing you want more than to have this Jesus in your life.

This is what happened while we were in Salt Lake City.

The day we were there, we met a man who had been a Christian missionary to the Mormons of Salt Lake City for about twenty years. He stood here and there in the city and railed against Joseph Smith, the founder of Mormonism, and the faith he founded. He preached the gospel of Jesus and exhorted the lost to be saved.

At first, I admit, I saw this man as somewhat of an adversary to us because he opposed what we did. He was one of those people who said God doesn't move in power today. By the end of our day there, however, I came to realize that this man's ministry was just as legitimate as ours. But But our method of going on the street to pray for people to experience the Holy Spirit had more fruit in one day than our missionary friend had had in twenty years.

If anyone's methods of ministry should be questioned, I think it should be those who simply try to talk people into believing. If we really care about Jesus' glory reaching far and wide across the earth, shouldn't we look more at the fruitfulness of a ministry rather than whether the people using it act with confidence that God is going to move on someone?

## God Is Not Afraid

What I saw on the streets that day shook me up. I think that was the point. Not only to shake me up, but to shake up the church and any observers.

*Holy Ghost* was designed from the get-go to make everybody who sees it uncomfortable at some point. I did that on purpose.

When I started editing my movie, I knew I had to make two separate films. So I asked the Lord how he wanted to do it.

Right away he spoke to me about the first film, saying, "Don't hold back. Push hard."

I said, "Okie-dokie." And that's why *Holy Ghost* is the way it is. It shows God's power and shows him breaking—sometimes destroying—the boxes we put him in. It shows that our God is not afraid.

Even if Will and Jamie went overboard a little bit, at the end of the day they were just trying to give people an experience with the living God so that they would choose a relationship with the living God.

God is a lot more forgiving and patient with us than most of the church is. Even if his kids get a little overexuberant, he can still use it to do whatever he wants. And God can choose to not show up if he doesn't like how you're doing something.

I think far too many people in churches are worried about

believers being overexuberant. We should be more concerned about a general under-exuberance for this incredibly extravagant, wondrous God we call Father. If you're going to err on one side or the other, why not err on having too much enthusiasm instead of too little?

We ought to be celebrating the people who are stepping out in faith, not criticizing them and calling them false prophets with counterfeit spirits.

God has not changed. He is still the powerful God of the Bible who did amazing signs and wonders. We don't have to wait for him to sovereignly move in power in someone's life. He sent us to be his instruments of reconciliation, helping an orphaned world return to its Father.

We can learn to discern what is real and what is fake, what is demonic and what is God. But we can't do that just by looking at whether spiritual power is used or by looking at the methods of ministry someone uses. We can't judge spiritual things by their outward appearance. We have to look deeper, and we have to look longer. What is the fruit of the ministry? Do these people proclaim Jesus? Are they setting people free? Do they accomplish the same things Jesus did in his ministry? These are the questions we need to ask.

If the church could get on the same page in this area, we would see a powerful wave of God's witnesses released into the world. It could unleash a people who don't care about whether they are overexuberant, but realize that they are standing between a lost world and the hell that waits for them if no one does something.

God is bigger than our religious bickering about how we minister. He's bigger than the boxes we've tried to put him in. He is waiting for us to join him in a wild world where his power reaches out to save the lost. I want to be with him, even when it's uncomfortable. How about you?

five

# God Is Untaintable

*God is not afraid of the dark; he knows his light overcomes it. God is not afraid of sin; he knows his righteousness transforms us. In fact, God isn't afraid of anything. So why are we? Christians too often use being "in the world but not of it" as an excuse to run and hide. But when we see how powerful the light we carry is, we will want to invade the darkness and watch as God's light changes lives everywhere we go.*

My most important rule as I create my movies is to pray before doing anything. I'm not talking about starting with a plan, then taking it to God and asking if it's a good idea. I would only do something if God told me to do it (or at least I *thought* he was telling me to do it). Since the Holy Spirit created the entire world, I let him direct my movies entirely and completely—except once.

In Rome, when I was filming with Todd White, Todd asked me to introduce him to Brian "Head" Welch, a guitarist and founding member of the heavy-metal band Korn. He had come to Jesus, and I was friends with him. Before Todd came to Jesus, he was in a metal band.

"I'm sure he'd love to meet you," I said. And then I had a sudden thought. *What if I took Todd to a Korn concert? That would be amazing!*

I asked him, "Would you be willing to film at a Korn concert?" Todd didn't have to think twice. "I'm in!"

"Okay. Well, let me talk to Brian." When I got home, I called Brian, told him what I was thinking of doing, and asked what he thought about it.

"That sounds terrifying, but let's do it."

## My Personal Rabbit Hole

You may think that going to a heavy-metal concert is about as dark and secular as you can get. Why would we even entertain the idea?

A few years back, when I was wrapping up filming on *Finger of God*, I was in Turkey with a large group of ministry leaders. Heidi Baker, a world-changing missionary to Mozambique, got up during these leaders' final dinner and announced to everyone that I was done with my filming after this trip. Then she had them all gather around me to pray for me and bless what I was doing.

When Heidi started to pray for me, everything was normal. But all of a sudden she stopped and quietly said, "Oh my. Oh dear."

I looked at her and asked, "What's going on?"

"I don't know how else to tell you this, so I'm just going to describe what I see. I see you filming the demonic. I see you filming the occult."

I gulped. "Is that a good thing or a bad thing?"

"I don't know."

She said she saw me filming, but I was done with that. I was going back to my family, my home, my students, my job. And was filming occult and demonic things even okay?

A lot of people—even people who believe in personal prophetic words today—would reject a word like that simply because it involves going into the darkness.

I told Heidi, "A word like this lights something inside me. There's a lot more to the story than what I thought I was filming."

You see, the English classes I taught at college were about how to form and write a story, and I thought *Finger of God* was the whole story. What more was there to say?

Because of the word Heidi gave me, I began to wonder if God might have more story to tell me and more for me to tell.

A couple of months later, at a church in Toronto, God showed me I needed to go into the most difficult spiritual climates to discover and show what his love really looks like.

At that point I had the beginning of a concept for my second movie, *Furious Love*, where I set out to do everything I could to test the limits of God's love. To do that, I had to find the darkest and most despicable places on earth, take God's love there as best as I could, and see what would happen.

## Try to Find God's Limits

Of course, my films go far beyond a Korn concert. We're talking about witchcraft festivals in Salem, Massachusetts, the brothels of Thailand where children are sold for profit, and Hindu temples dedicated to the goddess of death.

But more important, we're talking about the power of God's love. We are asking, "Is there a limit to where God can reach? Can someone find a darkness so deep that God cannot get to them? Can someone fall so far that he doesn't love them?"

I didn't film some of the darkest places on the planet for entertainment. I did it because I needed to know for myself how real and how powerful God's love is. I had to settle for myself a truth that long ago stopped feeling powerful. I grew up in church hearing,

"God loves you," but I heard it so much, day in and day out, that it stopped having meaning to me. More than anything else, I wanted that truth to mean something to me again.

To do that, I had to put God's love to the test, and being a skeptic, I had to make sure it was a really good test. I wanted to find the most lost people in the world, line them up, and say, "Okay, God, let's see you love these people."

What we discovered blew me away. I mean, of course we found that the darker a place was, the more brightly his light shone. But what really stood out to me was God's patience.

I went to the city dump in Madrid, where there were heroin addicts everywhere. I saw people at the end of their rope, desperate for their lives to change. They were miserable beyond anything we could imagine. Yet when they were presented with a way out—offered a God who can forgive their mess and their mistakes, a God who fully presents to them true love—they still denied him. They didn't want to give up their addiction.

I met a man in Thailand who was there specifically for the brothels. He wanted to have sex with little boys. That was his only reason to travel there. He paid thousands of dollars in airfare, hotel, and visas—just to rape little boys. The dad in me wanted to see this guy arrested and punished. But at the same time I realized that God actually loved this man. He wanted to bring him out of the addiction that controlled his life. This man wanted sex, but he didn't have love. What he needed was God's love.

As I filmed the darkness, the demonic, and the occult, that is what stood out to me the most—the fact that God loves us even in our depravity. That blew me away because I think most of us look at God through the lens of already being saved. Our lives are cleaned up now, at least more than they were when God saved us, or maybe we've always lived in the church world and our lives never really needed cleaning up. It's like, "We're good people now." Yeah, we screwed up years ago, but we're so far removed from those times that we've forgotten how God loved us before we were good, before we were nice and cleaned up.

God isn't going to walk away from these guys I met. He won't walk away from the heroin addict who spits rejection in God's face when he's offered the chance at a new life. God won't walk away from the pimps who sell children for profit, or the people who spend thousands of dollars to travel to the other side of the world to victimize boys and girls. He will pursue them for the rest of their lives because he loves them.

Now, those people still need to choose God in return at some point. At the end of the day, they need to say yes to him. But God will always be patient. Nothing they do, and nothing we do, could ever break his patience or push away his love.

## The Veil Is Torn

I haven't figured out why people have such an issue with Christians going to dark places, or even staying in dark places, because I'm not sure how else God's light is going to shine there. But I think some of it may come from seeing how God related to Israel in the Old Testament.

God taught Israel some pretty extreme things about holiness. He told them that there are holy things and there are defiled things. He taught them that if they touched a defiled thing, they became defiled. Then he powerfully drove this principle home by telling them to kill every man, woman, and child who belonged to the pagan nations inhabiting the Promised Land. He knew the people who worshiped demons would become a snare to his people and that they would become defiled—the very opposite of his intent to raise them into becoming his holy priesthood (Exodus 19:6).

Ezekiel took the point even further when he wrote about the visions God gave him of the temple in Jerusalem. While Ezekiel was in exile in Babylon, God showed him what was happening far away at the temple. He saw rulers, priests, and the leaders of society mocking God, saying surely he wouldn't see what they did in secret. They built altars to demons and worshiped them right there in the courts of the temple, filling the house that was set apart for worshiping the Lord with the worship of worthless idols. God showed Ezekiel that he'd had enough. And Ezekiel watched the cloud of God's presence lift from the Holy of Holies and leave Israel completely.

Maybe it's this kind of narrative that has Christians today protesting when believers take their light into dark places. But we need to look at the whole of Scripture to find how we should live today. If we don't, we might think we need to follow God's command to Joshua and kill those who carry darkness instead of converting them to the light.

Jesus humbled himself by laying aside the glories of heaven and being equal to God (Philippians 2:5–7). When Jesus became a man, he gathered disciples and wandered with them throughout the Israeli countryside, teaching them and doing miracles as they went along. At one point, they were in a place called Caesarea Philippi.

There was a cave in this region that people knew as the Gates of Hell. It was at the base of a giant rock face, with a smaller hill descending from it.

This cave had been a place of frequent human sacrifice to a god named Pan. This religion was straight-up worship of demons. The people believed they needed to make human sacrifices until blood ran out of the mouth of the cave and down the hill. Then their god would be satisfied and they wouldn't face its wrath. So they kept sacrificing humans—including children—until death literally filled the cave.

Whether or not that place was the Gates of Hell before those sacrifices, it sounds like a sure way to make that cave into a gateway to hell. Do you think Jesus was ignorant of what happened there when he chose to visit? Or do you think he knew the darkness there and chose to go anyway?

We know that he understood what he was doing, because while he was there he asked his disciples who people said he was. After hearing their answers, he asked them who they thought he was. Peter declared that he was the Christ, the Son of the Living God. Then Jesus uttered these powerful words: "Blessed are you, Simon Bar-Jonah! For flesh and blood has not revealed this to you, but my Father who is in heaven. And I tell you, you are Peter, and on this rock I will build my church, and the gates of hell shall not prevail against it" (Matthew 16:17–18).

Jesus went right to the place on earth that was known as the Gates of Hell and then declared he would build his church on that spot (symbolically, not physically). Jesus—the very presence of God with man—went to one of the darkest places in the world and didn't blink. Instead, he promised that the church he would build would never need to fear the darkness, for the very gates of hell could never overcome it.

Jesus went to the cross, facing every spirit of darkness, and died once and for all for every sin that had ever kept us from him. At that moment, the veil in the temple that protected the priests from God's manifest presence was torn from top to bottom: God's declaration that what separated man from God was now finished. His light shone out in the darkness, and the darkness could not overcome it (John 1:5).

During the next three days on earth, when it looked like death and darkness had won, Jesus was busy proclaiming life to imprisoned spirits (1 Peter 3:18–19) and rising to heaven with a host of captives in his wake (Ephesians 4:8–9) before finally rising physically from his tomb. Even when darkness seemed strongest, light's victory was just beginning to enforce its firm grip over eternity.

After his resurrection, Jesus commissioned his followers, backing them with all authority in heaven and earth. In the years that followed, Peter shone God's light to the Gentiles for the first time in history. Paul took the gospel to Athens, where so many demonic altars filled the city that he found one dedicated to the Unknown God. He turned that altar into his pulpit to preach salvation to every demon-worshiping pagan within reach of his voice.

Those disciples took the gospel to cities famous for their temple prostitutes, just like Thailand today. They proclaimed Jesus' lordship to emperors who thought they were gods. They braved riots. They dueled sorcerers and overpowered them.

Time and time again, they took light into the darkness. They lived Isaiah 60:1–2, "Arise, shine, for your light has come, and the glory of the LORD has risen upon you. For behold, darkness shall cover the earth, and thick darkness the peoples; but the LORD will arise upon you, and his glory will be seen upon you." Yes, darkness covered the earth, but they went right into that darkness to arise and shine because they understood that was where God's light belonged.

The veil between God and man really is torn. God's light shines in the darkness, and the darkness cannot overcome it. The day of being defiled by the darkness around us is past. Jesus' victory on our behalf is complete and sure.

This doesn't mean we are callous to it or unaware of how the devil can ensnare us in darkness if we give him an opportunity. It simply means we have more confidence in God's power than in the devil's! We believe our Father is good, loving, and powerful enough to protect us when we go as his ambassadors to those trapped in darkness, and that when his light shines on them, they will be transformed. They will be changed by the light; we will not be changed by the darkness.

## Getting Practical

It's great to tell hero stories from the Bible to show how light is stronger than darkness and that we shouldn't be afraid of taking the light we carry into any place on earth. But what does this actually look like? Well, let me tell you how I've handled these things in the past. Really, it all boils down to lots of prayer.

People ask me all the time, "What's it like to go into all those dark places? It must be really oppressive."

I usually tell them, "No, it really isn't. It's like walking into a museum." But I'm not a feeler. I know some people who have a keen supernatural sense of the unseen world around them. That's not me. I'm usually oblivious to spiritual dynamics going on around me in these places.

In all the traveling I've done and places I've filmed, there's only one time when I really thought, *Wow, this is a beast.* It's when I went to Thailand. We were going there to film in the heart of the global sex trade, and we'd heard that two months before we got there, some guy had been caught filming with a cell phone camera in one of the brothels. When the Russian mafia who runs this place caught that kid, they took him up on the roof and threw him off, killing him. We weren't coming in with little cell phone cameras. We were bringing in big, full-size, digital film cameras.

Obviously, we had a lot of people praying for our safety.

But four guys going to film for a week in the heart of the sex trade didn't exactly please our wives at home. We were going to be around scantily clad prostitutes whose job was to try to seduce us 24/7 for the entire week we were there. The whole city is an extremely sexualized place. Sex is all around, everywhere you look, throughout the entire red-light district.

So we set the tone for ourselves right away. We decided to meet every night to pray and talk with each other.

With all that diligence on our part, and support in prayer from around the world, the grace we had on us while we were there was amazing. Every single girl I looked at, no matter how beautiful—and they were beautiful—I felt like I was looking at my sister. No matter how beautiful your sister might be, even if you see her in a bathing suit, you're not attracted to her. It's actually repulsive to think of your sister sexually. God put us in such a grace bubble while we were in Thailand, that's what it was like the whole week.

On the last day we were there, the grace level started to lift. We didn't even want to go back to our hotel room. We just wanted to get out of there because we started to hate the whole place. I think the Lord was reminding us, "Hey, don't forget how much you need me for this film."

There's never any contest between light and dark; light wins every time. There is never a time when you flip the light switch in a dark room and the dark keeps the light from making the room bright.

## Cause a Ruckus

That's why I didn't think twice about taking Todd White to a Korn concert. The only problem was, I broke my rule when I decided to do it, because I didn't ask God first whether it's what he wanted me to do.

Nevertheless, we made the plans. We picked which concert to attend. We scheduled the trip. My idea to keep a controlled environment was to utilize the tour bus. I figured we'd get two or three big-time Korn fans before the concert, bring them back to the tour bus to meet Brian, and once we were all in the bus, we'd hit them with the Holy Spirit. Sounded like a great idea to me.

When we got to the tour buses, I introduced Todd and Brian. Fieldy, the bass player, also a Christian, joined us. While they talked, I sat there, looking around and thinking, *This is never going to work.* The tour bus was small and dark. There was no way to bring extra people back there and have room to do anything. I started to panic. And, finally, pray.

*All right, Lord, what do I do?*

I heard the Lord say, *Oh, now you're ready to ask me?* It wasn't mean. It just sounded like a chiding father saying, "Oh, now you want my advice?"

I prayed, *Yes. I'm so sorry. Please tell me what to do, because I have to make a decision in like five minutes.*

God spoke clearly. *I want you to take them out to the crowd and cause a ruckus.*

That didn't seem like a good idea. So I said, *Lord, I don't think Brian and Fieldy are going to like that because we don't really have security. And most people are in line already.*

About that moment, Brian stopped talking to Todd, turned to me, and said, "Okay, Mr. Director, what do you want to do?"

I took a deep breath. "Well, I don't know if you're going to like this. But I think I'm supposed to take you guys out to the crowd and start praying for people."

Brian stared at me. "Dude, last night I had a dream, and that's exactly what we did. If you didn't mention that idea to me, I was going to suggest that's what we do."

The Lord was clearly directing this movie. So that's what we did. We went out to the crowd waiting in line to get into the show, and we prayed. Even while we were filming, it was electric.

## Let God Be God

What most people get upset about isn't that we went to a Korn concert, or even that we filmed there, as long as we did it to pray for people and see God touch them. What they get really upset about is that Brian and Fieldy remain in that world. That's a real stumbling block for some people. They say, "How can they call themselves Christians, yet keep spewing forth these filthy lyrics, being a part of this culture that's dark and, in some cases, demonic?"

I get it. But because I'm friends with Brian and I've talked at length with him about this stuff, I don't get it.

He quit the band when he got saved, and he was out of the band for close to ten years. He only went back when he felt the Lord telling him, *You're made for this, and you can handle all this that's going to get thrown at you, because I'm with you now.*

So whenever people ask me, "How can he be in that environment?" I say, "Well, what's the alternative? Would you prefer there to be no Christian presence in that environment and just let everybody go to hell? Because who else is going to reach them?"

When we were backstage, Brian pointed out all the roadies who travel with them, and almost all of them had become believers. And when Todd and I did this with Brian and Fieldy, it lit a fire inside them and gave them a boldness they never had before.

When they went on their next tour, they brought a pastor friend with them. His job was to go out into the crowd during the concerts and look for people he felt the Holy Spirit was highlighting. He usually went up to about 100 to 125 people and invited them to meet Brian and Fieldy after the show.

At every concert, more than a hundred kids came to this meeting after the show, where Brian and Fieldy gave their testimonies and then invited people to receive Jesus.

Now, kids who go to a Korn concert are angry and hurt. Brian says, "This is my tribe. I understand them because that's where I come from." He's reaching back to his people. And thousands of kids are getting saved at Korn concerts, simply because Brian and Fieldy decided to trust God to be with them in that environment, to believe that God's light in them would be stronger than the darkness around them.

I get that many people are uncomfortable with these things. But look at the fruit that's coming from it. Consider how many kids are having encounters with Jesus and getting saved, getting called out of their lives of anger and pain.

I think if we're offended by things like this, we're going to just have to get over ourselves. There comes a point where we have to let God be God.

And he's not afraid of darkness. Or our sin.

Brian rejoined Korn when he heard God say he'd be with him. When I was in Thailand, I could tell when God was with me, and I knew the grace bubble we walked in was because so many people prayed for us.

What might happen if, instead of bashing or judging or second-guessing those people who invade dark places, we prayed for them? It could make all the difference in their ability to walk in God's grace and power. And instead of judgment getting thrown everywhere, people would be getting saved as God's light invades the darkness and overcomes it.

# six

# God Is Pure

*The natural world can be a complicated one. It's hard to know who to trust and who's in it for themselves. This remains true when the spiritual world is part of our situation, even within the church. The trick is to figure out how to discern the genuine from the charlatan, the pure from the selfish. Thankfully, a little experience can save us from cynicism and introduce us to some of the best people in the world.*

When you film things, you get a chance to see the very best and the very worst in people. It wasn't that way when I started, but the increased visibility that came with each movie's success drew countless ministers and ministries out of the woodwork, each with their own agenda.

I wish I could say that every minister out there is genuine and trustworthy. But that simply isn't true. There are a lot of insecure ministers out there who grasp at anything they think will make them feel significant. And there are a lot of ministers who are just looking to promote themselves, to take advantage of any situation they can to put themselves forward.

The good news is, there are more good people out there doing good things than you might expect. And they're pretty easy to recognize once you know what to look for. I've had the privilege of meeting a number of wonderful people all over the world, and these people all have something in common. As you read the following stories, it will become clear to you.

## Francis Was Dead

When you're a skeptic, you're always wondering whether people are telling you the truth. This was never truer for me than when I was filming *Finger of God*. Things I had thought were true were proven false, and things I had thought were false were proven true.

In the middle of filming the movie, I traveled to Mozambique for the first time to see Heidi Baker in action. I had heard of all the miracles she'd seen God do, including raising the dead. When I researched more about her, I discovered that resurrections from the dead were not unusual for Heidi or for the ministers she and her husband, Rolland, had raised up in Africa.

Now, for a skeptic, it's an amazing opportunity when your journey takes you to a place where you can meet people who are actually purported to have come back from the dead.

As I prepared to visit Heidi, I asked her if I could talk to any of these resurrected people while I was there. She said, "There might be one. I'll ask him if he's willing to meet with you."

Sure enough, Heidi arranged for a man named Francis to meet with me in Johannesburg during my four-hour layover there on my way to Mozambique. And he told me his story.

Francis was at church one night. His job was to welcome people as they came through the gate. But when it got late, he decided to close and lock the gate. At the last minute, four men approached him. Thinking they wanted to come in to the church meeting, he welcomed them. Instead of joining the others inside the church, they beat Francis to death.

A few people in the church found an old car and took Francis's body to the hospital while the rest of the congregation remained behind to pray for him. After about an hour of praying, Francis's dead body at the hospital suddenly came alive.

Although Francis was miraculously alive, he was still terribly injured from the beating and had what looked like a long road of recovery ahead. Before the hospital put him to sleep for the night, he managed to whisper, "Forgive them." These words made it back to the church, where the police, who had caught one of the murderers, were trying to get someone to sign papers to press charges.

The church refused to press charges. As soon as they issued this united forgiveness, the hospital called the church to say, "Come pick up your guy. There's nothing wrong with him." There was not one scratch on his body, not one bruise. He could see and speak perfectly.

Francis went from the hospital to the police station, where he asked to see the man who had killed him. He urged the police to release the man because he had forgiven him. When the police refused, Francis persisted, insisting that his murderer didn't know what he was doing.

When the police finally released Francis's attacker, Francis hugged him. He called him his brother and told him God loved him, that all he wanted was that he would receive Jesus and go home happy.

The man did receive Jesus, and then he went to Bible school. Today he tells everyone he can how God changed the heart of a murderer through the forgiveness of a dead man.

After I finished filming Francis telling his amazing story, I asked where he was from, figuring that he must be from Johannesburg since that's where he came to meet me. Turns out he had driven five hours to get to our ten o'clock meeting. He'd gotten up early to drive five hours just to tell his story to a stranger, then drive five hours back home.

If people in the West are willing to travel that long to meet someone, they bring their business cards, a book (or two or three), and promotional material. Then they give a sales pitch. Francis has no book. He has no ministry he's trying to promote. He didn't leave me with a website where people can find him to donate money to his cause.

So I asked him, "Why would you wake up at four in the morning to meet me?"

"Because you asked me to," he said, as if it were no big deal. "And because Heidi asked."

This man wasn't out to get anything for himself. He just wanted Jesus to be famous.

"If this is going to bring people to Jesus," Francis told me, "then I want to do it."

There was absolutely nothing fake about him. He was pure through and through.

## A Woman Who Gets Younger

Shortly after I met with Francis, I got on the airplane to finish traveling to Heidi's home in Pemba, Mozambique. While I stayed with her, she said to me, "You know, everybody is growing older, but spiritually, I want to grow younger. I want to be as much a child as possible because Jesus said, 'Such a one as this receives the kingdom.'" She truly lives that way. She operates with the faith of a child.

I could write a whole book about the faith of Heidi Baker. What she and her husband have done and all the miracles they've seen by walking in faith over the years is incredible. But I was still a baby in all that stuff when I went out there to film with her. At one point I told her, "I wonder if anything is going to happen when we go out," expressing doubt that God would work miracles in my presence.

She laughed. "Of course stuff is going to happen!"

"How can you be so sure?"

"Because that's what God does! He likes to touch his kids. He never doesn't show up."

We went out to a remote village. After showing the Jesus film, she invited people to receive Jesus, and the children of the village did. Then Heidi called for all the deaf and blind to come to her. One deaf woman came forward. Everyone in the village knew her. The children prayed, God came, and the woman was healed. Her hearing was restored.

At the time, again, I was a college professor, trying to figure out if I even believed in the miraculous. And there I was, watching people get healed by children who had just come to Jesus two minutes before. I watched a woman who was deaf get her hearing.

When you're skeptical, even if you're with someone who sees miracles happen all the time, you wonder if God is going to do anything miraculous. But when you see miracles with your own eyes, you say to yourself, *Of course God could do something like this. It's all over the Bible!*

All of this came from a simple, childlike saint who describes herself as "one little woman in the dirt." Yes, this woman travels to speak all over the world, and she does have a book she sells. She came from a wealthy family. She was born into privilege and lived well by the world's standards her whole life, even getting a doctorate in theology from King's College in London. But she left all that thirty years ago to move to a war-torn country that, at the time, was one of the worst on the planet.

When Heidi moved to Mozambique, the country was in the

middle of a coup to throw off Portuguese rule. Once that goal was accomplished, the nation moved into a civil war where genocide-like atrocities were a normal way of life. Land mines were scattered everywhere, and innocents often unwittingly discovered them. Unemployment was 90 percent, making it one of the world's worst economies.

That was when Rolland and Heidi moved their young family there. They decided to spend their lives helping a people who were doing nothing for themselves but harm, who were horribly oppressed by the spirit of death and destruction.

Thirty years later, Heidi cares for ten thousand orphans every day. She travels to third-world villages where she regularly sees the entire population receive Jesus. She has started a university in Mozambique that is growing into one of the finest institutions in all of Africa. Her reach goes far beyond one African nation, as she has opened mission bases and orphanages in many other nations around the world. Any finances she receives from speaking fees or book sales are not going to enrich her in a worldly sense, but are being poured into the poorest of the poor. She is changing the world as we know it.

Heidi is one of many people I have met who have an incredible purity about them. She wants to see God move, not so she can build her own ministry kingdom, but just to reach more people. Even though God is lifting her up, if you took her out to dinner, you would walk away impressed by how much she loves Jesus and wants him to be famous. The same is true about Francis and many other people I've met while making my films. The higher God lifts them, the higher they lift him.

The reason they have such major ministries is that they have pure hearts. They care more about Jesus being glorified than about themselves being glorified.

## Ignore the Wrong Kind

Meeting amazing people like Francis or Heidi helps me do what we all need to do with the stories we hear of people who made huge mistakes or caused scandals—ignore them. Don't let them get under your skin, and certainly don't let them shake your faith.

I know that when some people hear about a big-name minister who may be a fake, they think, *You just can't believe anything.* I know what that's like. As a skeptic, I've questioned beliefs in more ways than the average person.

I've had plenty of reasons to question my faith because of what I have seen in ministry. People I have filmed who've flamed out or become so weird that I can't point others to them anymore. I've had trust broken. I've been closer to some leaders' failures than most Christians.

People send me videos all the time and say, "Hey, our ministry is doing this amazing thing. You should come film it." I never film those people because they just tipped their hand. They may think they have pure hearts, but anyone who tells me, "Come highlight what we're doing," is not who I'm looking for.

Many people are out to promote themselves more than Jesus. But there are also a lot of people who are the real deal. Because of my experiences, I'm able to deal with the doubt that sometimes comes when my faith is buffeted by someone else's failure.

Let's say you were trying to learn how to hit a golf ball. You hit the ball ten times, and all ten times it's terrible. You might say, "I stink. I'll never be good at this." But if you hit it right a couple of times, you'll think, *I can do this because I've done it before.*

When you have experience with what's real, of how things should be, that creates a mind-set in you that success is possible. I think that's why God tells us so many times in Scripture to renew our minds every day. He's always telling us to remember the great things he's done for us, because it's in that remembrance that we build up our faith again.

If we think about the genuine, pure-hearted people out there who love Jesus and simply want to make him famous, we won't be shaken when another person falls, even when it's someone we trusted and looked up to. We can't let ourselves focus on the mountain in front of us, forgetting all the mountains God has lain waste behind us.

## The Ones with Pure Hearts

When I filmed *Father of Lights* with Mike and Deena Van't Hul, they really impressed me.

Mike and Deena used to be typical Western Christians. He was vice president of a bank, and they had a big home, nice cars, and everything anyone could want. But their faith was lukewarm, and they weren't very active in their church. They wondered whether there was more to living for Jesus than they knew.

Randy Clark came to their church as a guest speaker and invited the Holy Spirit to touch the people there. All over the room, people fell down under the power and presence of God, including Mike and Deena. They were only down for a short time, but when they got up they were completely transformed.

They sold their house, gave away everything they had, and moved with their three young children to China, taking only a couple of suitcases of clothes with them. They had no plans or connections, and they didn't know the language. All they knew was that God had told them to do this and they were following him.

After three days in a hotel, they found an apartment to rent that had rats and open sewage. Not a glamorous beginning.

They miraculously formed key relationships, and doors opened for them to establish an orphanage specifically for children who were blind, lame, disabled, or disfigured. The lowest of the low, the kids no one else wanted.

They provided a safe place for children who had been stolen from their parents and kids who had experienced abuse. They held children while they died in their arms. Though they did all this with almost no monthly support, every month God miraculously provided for their financial needs.

As soon as I heard about these guys, I thought, *I have to film them.* When I called them, I discovered that they're huge fans of my films. They'd even watched the deluxe editions and special features.

I told them, "Hey, I want to come film you guys, to highlight what you're doing. I want to show the world what you've been up to."

Their first response was hesitation. "We're going to have to pray about this," Mike said.

I thought, *What's there to pray about?* But I said okay and waited for their answer.

Several days later, Mike called back and said yes, but he sounded very reluctant. "We've felt the Lord telling us to do this, but we don't really want to. We're concerned that people will be moved to the point where they feel compelled to help us financially, and we don't want to lose our need to have faith that God will provide."

It was like they had become addicted to having faith and they didn't want to lose that because it was such a sweet place for them.

The whole time I was with them, they kept making comments like, "I still don't know if we should be doing this."

There couldn't be a clearer picture of the kind of people I like to film with, or even just be with. It was almost like a sacrifice to them to have attention brought to their ministry. This kind of person is clearly not in it for money, or for fame, or to make people like them, or for any other reason that has anything to do with them. They are simply doing it because God told them to, because his love is the greatest pursuit of their lives. Their obedience to that pursuit led to my being blessed to meet them and film with them.

## This Isn't Hollywood

I frequently get called a charlatan. I've been accused of exploiting situations for money; the people I film get that too.

If the movies I make weren't changing people's lives, I never would have left being a college professor. But I don't really care about me. I care about the people I film with, the people I carefully searched for, the ones I traveled to and met with and looked right in the eye.

I could film just about anyone. It's easy to get people to say yes to me. But I weed through a constant bombardment of opportunities to find people who have character. How can anyone seriously conclude that people like Francis, Heidi, or Mike and Deena are promoting anyone except Jesus?

I take my job seriously. I take the influence that God has given me seriously. I want to be like the heroes I've described in this chapter, lifting God as high as I can and shouting his name louder than anything else, no matter how high God might lift me.

Unlike Hollywood, nothing in my movies is fake. The people I film have no aspirations of becoming celebrities and in many cases work to avoid notoriety.

I know there are charlatans out there, but should that be the focus of our lives? Should we hunt down all the people we think are fake and then attack them? Is that really going to build God's kingdom?

Maybe what we should do instead is fix our eyes on what is pure, like Paul teaches us to do in Philippians 4:8. As we do that, let's cherish the people God brings across our path who have pure hearts. And allow them to change us so that we become pure hearted as well.

Then God will have a lot more people he can use to make himself famous throughout the world.

# seven

# God Is the Same to Everyone

*The stories I share in movies can be inspiring, just knowing that God is working powerfully through a variety of people all over the world. Many Christians, however, hear stories of God at work and think he could never use them that way because they aren't super-Christians. The truth is, there are no super-Christians. There are only normal people who have said yes to God.*

I'm amazed at all God has done since I started filming. He's taken me from being a curious college professor to traveling the world trying to discover the truth about miracles. This is what God does. He takes us from where we are to places far beyond what we could ever imagine. He starts with our little, and then gives us much, if we just say yes to him and follow him.

Maybe it's the Hollywood element that seems to come with the making of any kind of film, but I get a lot of feedback saying that the people I film look like super-Christians. Sometimes people even think I'm one. While these people are inspired that God is working miracles through various people, they are convinced that God could never do such things through them.

What good does it do the body of Christ (and a world full of lost people) if God's greatest works are reserved for a handful of super-Christians? For the sake of a body in need of God's miracles, and a world in even greater need of them, God is raising all of us up to become miracle workers. The supernatural isn't for a small group of super-Christians; it's for everyone.

## Heidi's Children

Telling stories about Heidi Baker may seem to be the wrong way to prove my point that the supernatural is for everyone. But you'd be surprised how many miracles people associate with Heidi that God actually did through much less notable hands.

When Heidi decides to plant a new church, she looks for some remote village that is completely unreached. In many cases, these villages are predominantly Muslim. If they aren't Muslim, they are heavily steeped in some pagan worship system like voodoo. She drives to the village with a portable generator, movie projector and screen, sound system, and sometimes a small stage. In almost every village, just the presence of these things will draw a crowd.

When the setup is done, she shows the Jesus film. Many of these villages have never heard of Jesus, so the film is a great way to introduce him to them. Afterward, she says, "This Jesus is real and I'll prove it to you. But first, who wants him right now?"

Nine times out of ten, all the children raise their hands because they already believe. So she calls up the children who just heard about Jesus for the first time and accepted him only seconds before. Once they come to her, she says, "Now bring me your sick. Bring me your deaf and blind. The lepers and the lame. Bring the worst that you have, and I will prove to you that Jesus is real."

Every village accepts the challenge and brings their most hopeless cases. But Heidi does not lay hands on any of them. Instead she has the children do it. When these children, who just accepted Jesus, lay hands on the sick, blind, lame, deaf, mute, and leprous, 100 percent of them are healed. When the village witnesses such incredible miracles, they all receive Jesus right then and there.

People think, *Well, Heidi has a great gift.* Of course, she does pray for people. But most of the time it's the little kids who just accepted Jesus, who know nothing about him but what they saw in a movie, who are participating in the healing miracles.

People all over the world travel to Pemba, Mozambique, to sit at Heidi's feet and learn from her, hoping that if they hang out with her, some of her super-Christian powers will rub off on them. Now, I'm not saying there isn't value in learning from people who are already doing what you want to do. But Heidi is a human being. In herself she has no power to do any of the things God has done through her. It has all been God!

Heidi has the same Holy Spirit you and I have. God doesn't love her more than he loves you. There's nothing special about her that makes her able to see miracles happen.

Some people would say, "Well, Heidi must have more faith. That must be why she sees so many miracles when other people struggle and don't get the same results." I have to disagree. Because I know myself.

## Faith Isn't the Issue

When I was working on *Furious Love*, one of Jeff Jansen's former students, a video guy, asked me to come to Africa and help him film the crusade. I thought, *Hey, that can start my movie.* So I agreed.

This was my first shoot after finishing *Finger of God*, so I was still raw in all this supernatural stuff. I was convinced that miracles were real; I believed in the supernatural. But I was just the guy behind the camera. That was where I was comfortable. I didn't want to pray for people. I just wanted to film other folks praying for people.

While we were in Africa to film the crusade, a group of men whom I'd consider to be professional ministers were going around to various towns in the area to pray for people and take whatever ministry opportunities they could stir up.

I went with them to a little village on a mountain, where we came upon a guy who had a lot of pain in his knee. These ministers all prayed for the guy, while I filmed it all, but nothing was happening.

One of the guys turned to me and said, "Hey, Darren, you want to pray for him?"

My first thought was, *Heck, no! If you guys can't heal him, I definitely can't. I barely believe in this stuff!*

At that point in my life I had never prayed aloud. And I had never prayed over anyone. My wife and I had gotten into arguments over it. She wanted me to pray for people at church, and I always refused, saying, "I don't do that." I wouldn't even pray with my wife.

But the camera was rolling, and people were looking at me. I didn't really have a choice. So I did the only thing I could do. I handed off my camera to the guy who was helping me. I just knew this was going to be super embarrassing.

I walked up to the man, knelt down, and put my hand on his knee. Then my mind went blank. I didn't know what to say or do. I couldn't even remember how to pray. Chalk it up to stage fright, but I couldn't think of anything.

I tried to remember things people had prayed while I filmed them. But nothing came to mind.

Finally, I kind of spilled out something like, "Lord, heal him." Then I sat there, staring at his knee, feeling like the biggest idiot. I was failing, on film, for everyone to see.

After a while, I decided I'd been down on my knees long enough. So I stood. Remembering that every time I'd filmed someone pray for healing, they always asked the person to test and see if they were healed, I said to the man, "Oh, you can test it now."

He stood and grinned. "It's 100 percent better. It's totally healed."

I was incredulous. All I could say was "Praise Jesus!"

A lot of people say you just need more faith to start seeing miracles happen in your life. But I had no faith at all. I couldn't even pray. I didn't expect anything to happen. But the man was healed.

Since then I've had moments when I've had complete faith that a person is going to be healed and nothing has happened. So I'm convinced it has nothing to do with our faith. I don't have a big part to play in someone's healing. I just pray. It's God who heals.

Whether or not a miracle happens has nothing to do with how much I've prayed or how long I've fasted. It has nothing to do with how great my devotions were that morning. Or how righteous my life has been. It has everything to do with whatever is happening in the Spirit.

Our job, then, is just to love people. And if there's an opportunity to bless someone and pray for healing, do it. If God doesn't heal them, don't take it as a personal failure. You succeeded simply by stepping out in faith to pray.

The pressure is off of us because we have no power to heal people anyway.

## Don't Stop at the Headlines

The people we might perceive to be super-Christians weren't always powerful prayer warriors. They all have their own stories of where they came from and how they got to where they are.

Most people who've seen my movies associate me with miracles. Many of them lump me into the category of super-Christians, those chosen by God to change the world. But without God, I am small and powerless.

I don't make headlines. I write headlines for others to broadcast the good news about how amazing God is. The point of the headlines is God. He's the one doing miracles. He alone has the power to save, heal, and deliver. He is the only star in all of my movies. Everyone you see him use and work through are just his servants. Those people are just like you.

Before I filmed *Furious Love*, I had never prayed for anyone in my life. Even after I made feature-length films about miracles, traveled all over the world, and saw many supernatural things firsthand, I was still the same man! Yet thanks to God's faithfulness to work in me, I made two movies strictly off the leading of the Holy Spirit. I'm not praising myself by any means. I'm simply saying that if I could grow like that, what's stopping you from stepping out and seeing what God will do? Even if you don't think it will work.

Many people who are known for their worldwide healing ministries prayed for hundreds of people before they saw their first miracle. Bill Johnson, a man I feature in all my films for his insight into the supernatural, pastors a church in California, and people travel from all over the world to hear him. But when he first became a pastor, he lost more than a thousand people from his church overnight.

I have only two reasons for ever telling their stories. The first reason is to brag on Jesus and how amazing and real he is. I never want anyone to walk away from one of my movies impressed by the people I filmed or by me. I want them to be impressed with Jesus.

The second reason is that I want people to be inspired to create their own stories. I want them to see how big God is, that he can use anyone who is willing to take the risk. All it takes is us saying yes.

No matter where you are right now, you don't need to clean up your life before giving it to God. We need God to do that for us. This is the gospel message that has been preached for years.

Christians seem to think that this truth only applies to people who need to get saved. So we tell this to unbelievers when we share the gospel with them. But we forget that it's still true for Christians after they get saved.

We cannot earn our way into being good enough for God to use us. We will never be qualified. We could never be worthy of the salvation God gives us in Jesus. How could we ever be good enough to earn his working through us in the lives of others?

But that's the point. God works with us and through us to build his kingdom. He leads us outside our comfort zone to help us grow. He doesn't leave us where he found us, but he matures us and leads us to new things.

## Pursue God, Not Greatness

Don't set out to be a super-Christian. Don't make it your purpose to grab headlines or get noticed. Don't even go a nobler route and say you want to change the world or make a big impact for Jesus. Just seek Jesus. Pursue him. Go after him. And then see what happens for you.

When we seek God, even if we're skeptically curious about how real he is today, he shows up. We draw near to him and he draws near to us. I never expected to see miracles, but I saw them anyway because I was seeking God.

Actually, I'm not sure I can say that I pursued God in the beginning. I pursued a mystery, and seeking the truth about that mystery turned out to be pursuing the truth about God. God counted that as good enough. He revealed that he is powerful, supernatural, and very real today. The more I saw of him, the more it changed me.

Don't expect God to move by himself. He usually waits for us to make the first move (see James 4:8). Too many people are waiting for God to sovereignly move on them, to sweep over them and transform their lives in a moment. That's not how it works.

The disciples prayed for ten days before the Holy Spirit fell on them at Pentecost (Acts 1–2). Cornelius set himself up for an encounter with the Holy Spirit through a devout life of generosity and prayer, even as a Gentile (Acts 10:1–2). Paul and Barnabas were sent out as missionaries for the first time while their church in Antioch pursued God (Acts 13:1–3). Over and over we see God drawing near to people as they seek him.

What made our biblical heroes great was God. Without him in the story, there is no happy ending. Goliath would have killed David. Noah would never have built an ark. Daniel would have been eaten by lions, if he'd lived long enough to get that far. And the walls of Jericho might still be standing today. God is the reason those stories happened. And it's the same with the incredible stories happening today.

## This Is Who God Is

Who God is never changes. He's the same yesterday, today, and forever. He's also not going to be one person to you and another person to me; he'll simply be himself with all of us.

God likes to work in partnership with humankind. We see it throughout history. As soon as God made Adam, he brought Adam into the process of creation by having him name the animals. God told Noah he planned to flood the earth, so he had Noah build a boat. God wanted to bless all the nations of the earth, so he promised Abraham he'd do that through him and his offspring. God told Moses, "I'm going to rescue my children, Israel, from their suffering in Egypt, therefore I am sending you."

I especially love that last example because God said he was going to rescue his people from Egypt. The exact quote is, "I have come down to deliver them out of the hand of the Egyptians and to bring them up out of that land to a good and broad land. ... Come, I will send you to Pharaoh that you may bring my people, the children of Israel, out of Egypt" (Exodus 3:8, 10).

Notice that God said he was the one who would deliver Israel from Egypt. Then God said Moses would bring his people out of Egypt. If I were in Moses' place, I'd be saying, "Whoa, wait a minute. You just said *you* were going to get them out of Egypt. Now you're saying *I'm* the one who's going to do it?"

I can imagine all the questions that must have gone through his head. *Why me? Why not someone else? Why do you even need help? Why don't you just show yourself to Pharaoh in a burning bush and talk to him? Why are you bringing me into this problem?*

Certainly, God didn't need Moses to help him. It's not like Moses had any strength or ability God lacked. None of the signs and wonders Moses did in Egypt came from his own abilities; it was all God's doing. God could have done those things on his own. He could have rescued his people in any number of ways, from killing all the Egyptians right from the start to simply turning Pharaoh's heart to let Israel go. But he didn't do any of those things. He chose to partner with Moses, and through Moses to invite all of Israel into partnership with him. Why? Because that's what he does. He builds partnerships with humankind.

Jesus shows us the same picture of God's nature. For three years, Jesus built momentum through his ministry. Multitudes followed him everywhere he went. He had years of experience leading large groups of people before he died. How much greater crowds could he have gathered after he rose from the dead? All of Israel knew he'd been crucified. Most of Israel probably witnessed his execution because it happened near a major highway into Jerusalem during a holiday that required the entire nation to celebrate by gathering there. They would have had to walk by his sacrifice in order to make the sacrifice God's laws required of them.

Any leader today would look at this opportunity as one that simply couldn't be missed. If you just show up, the whole world will notice. Your following and influence will immediately grow to unprecedented numbers. Jesus chose to partner with individual people instead. To paraphrase the Great Commission, he said, "I have all authority in heaven and earth, and with that authority, I choose to send you."

Every single person gathered on the mountain to hear Jesus speak those words had reason to question his judgment. Peter was a fisherman and had recently denied Jesus. Matthew was hated by his own people because he had been a tax collector. Thomas had doubted the resurrection just days before. Mary Magdalene had been a demon-possessed prostitute. These were Jesus' chosen partners to disciple the nations! Not one of them had international connections or successful leadership experience. None of them had ever managed a large group of people or had a teaching background. The only thing they had was him. And that was all that mattered.

It sounds a lot like the partners Jesus chooses today. Kris Vallotton was a mechanic recovering from a lifetime of abusive stepfathers. Todd White was a heavy-metal-rocking drug addict. And, like Thomas, I was a skeptic who doubted that the miracle I witnessed was genuine.

There's nothing you can do to disqualify yourself from Jesus' partnership. Paul had dedicated his life to murdering God's children, and Jesus still partnered with him.

There's nothing anyone could do to make him overlook you,

either. Daniel was raised in pagan Israel, castrated and taken captive, then forced to serve the nation that murdered his parents, yet God still partnered with him. Whether you knew it or not when you decided to start a relationship with Jesus, he's always looking for people like you and me to partner with him until all the nations see how good he is.

If you have a relationship with Jesus, he is looking to partner with you. The only question is whether you will say yes.

eight

# God Is
# Gracious

*Many people think you need to take a hard stand against*
*sin in order to prove you think righteous living is important.*
*They think evangelism has to confront unbelievers about*
*their sin or it's going soft. This belief simply doesn't under-*
*stand God's grace—his power to not just forgive a sinner but*
*to also transform him into a saint. The truth is that while*
*righteousness does matter, so does kindness, and in the end*
*it's God's kindness that leads sinners to repent.*

Not long ago I had my first encounter with picketers. I'd seen such people on the news, but I'd never had them come to one of my events to picket me!

I was on tour for the release of *Holy Ghost Reborn* when someone brought to my attention that picketers had gathered outside the building. While I was surprised, I thought it was pretty awesome that anyone would want to picket me.

I went out to talk to the picketers, thinking, *I want to meet these guys.* When I stepped out of the building, I saw a group of people with bullhorns and signs. I walked up to one of the guys, stuck out my hand, and said, "Hi. I'm Darren."

He narrowed his eyes at me. "Oh, I know who you are." He glared at my extended hand. "I'm not shaking your hand until you repent."

"What do I need to repent for?"

"You're lying to people by not telling them that if they don't repent of their sins they're going to burn in hell."

We stood there and talked for quite a while. I offered Scriptures to support my beliefs. He misquoted Scripture back to me. Obviously I wasn't going to get anywhere with this guy or his fellow picketers.

## Adversarial Evangelism Doesn't Work

I've had other run-ins with hard-line, fire-and-brimstone kinds of people all over the world who think I'm too easy on sin. It boils down to a stark contrast between their style of trying to reach the lost and mine. As with anything else, outward actions tell very little. But asking why our styles are so different will show us everything we need to know.

Some people think that to get people saved, you have to get them to repent of their sin. If they don't repent, they will burn in hell.

I think this is the wrong approach for a number of reasons. First, it's adversarial. You create a wall between yourself and the unbeliever, setting up an us-versus-them encounter. You argue, and they become defensive and fight back.

Stephen used this kind of language when he preached to the Sanhedrin in Acts 7, and it got him stoned—without converting a single person. Instead of trying to emulate his inflammatory style, we could learn from his example that argumentatively exposing people's sin isn't going to work. In fact, it almost always makes enemies.

Some people think everything in the Bible is prescriptive—it prescribes a particular way of living. If the hero of a story does a certain thing, people think we ought to do the same thing. In

Stephen's case, he's obviously the hero of his story. The fact that he was martyred makes him that much more of a hero. So people think we should do things the same way he did.

Certainly some books in the Bible do prescribe how we ought to live. Theologically heavy books like Paul's epistles fall into this category. But other books of Scripture aren't prescriptive; they simply tell stories. The point is, you can't treat all the books in the Bible the same way.

One story from Judges—a historical book—illustrates this point clearly. God raised up a judge named Jephthah to deliver Israel from the Ammonites. As with the other judges, Jephthah faced a great army, yet the Lord came upon him to lead him to overwhelming victory. The problem was that before going to battle, Jephthah made a vow that if the Lord gave him victory, he would offer whatever first came out of his door when he arrived home as a burnt sacrifice. I'm not sure what he expected to welcome him home, but what first walked out the door to greet him was his only child, a daughter. The two of them agreed he had to keep his vow, so Jephthah made a human sacrifice to the Lord (see Judges 10–11).

Now, if that story tells us how we ought to live our lives, then we have a conflict with the laws God gave to Moses that directly forbid human sacrifice. Obviously, God is not telling us to kill our own children. If anything, we should learn from Jephthah's mistake not to make rash vows.

Jephthah's story didn't end well, and neither did Stephen's. These men had the Spirit of God upon them, but that doesn't mean God inspired their words or their actions. You can't blame God for what happened to either Jephthah's daughter or to Stephen.

Arguing with unbelievers isn't going to get them saved. More often than not, it's going to make them feel like your enemy.

## God Isn't Angry Anymore

The second problem I have with the fire-and-brimstone approach to evangelism is that it portrays God as angry and vengeful. Yes, there are plenty of Scripture verses to show this side of God's nature. But Jesus died for our sins, and because of his sacrifice, God's wrath has been completely satisfied.

Therefore he had to be made like his brothers in every respect, so that he might become a merciful and faithful high priest in the service of God, to make *propitiation* for the sins of the people. (Hebrews 2:17)

My little children, I am writing these things to you so that you may not sin. But if anyone does sin we have an advocate with the Father, Jesus Christ the righteous. He is the *propitiation* for our sins, and not for ours only but also for the sins of the whole world. (1 John 2:1–2)

For all have sinned and fall short of the glory of God, and are justified by his grace as a gift, through the redemption that is in Christ Jesus, whom God put forward as a *propitiation* by his blood, to be received by faith. (Romans 3:23–25)

God's wrath built up because of the sins we committed, but through Jesus' sacrifice that wrath has been appeased. God no longer needs to punish people for their sins, because he already punished his Son, who sacrificed himself for their sake.

Each of these verses points out something important about how God views propitiation and therefore how we too should view it. The passage in Hebrews says that Jesus had to be made like you and me in every way or he couldn't fulfill his mission. Then it describes what his mission was—to extend mercy to the people by completely satisfying God's wrath. More than that, Jesus' mission of mercy is connected with his being faithful as a high priest to God.

The passage in 1 John makes a bold statement that Jesus didn't just pay for the sins of Christians, as some people teach, but that he paid for the sins of the whole world, whether they believe in him or not. Jesus paid for the sins of every person you will ever meet in your entire life, no matter how wicked and cruel they may be. He isn't waiting for them to repent before extending his blood over them on God's mercy seat. He already satisfied any anger God would ever have toward the world's sins.

If we stopped here it might sound like every single person is going to heaven. But that's not true. In Romans 3:23–25, Paul tells us how the truth and power of what Jesus has done for us becomes activated in our lives—by faith. Jesus has already redeemed everyone, justified everyone, and become the propitiation for everyone. But each of us needs to believe it. And as soon as we do, we instantly gain the benefit of what Jesus has done.

## Follow Jesus' Example

For people who still think they need to convince unbelievers that they are sinners by railing against their sins, there's a third issue I have with adversarial evangelism. It doesn't follow Jesus' example.

"Wait!" I can hear you saying. "Jesus yelled at people all the time." You're right. But the only people he ever yelled at were the religious elite who yelled at everyone else for not following the rules. He judged them by the same standard they used to judge everyone else. He gave them the same treatment they dished out. I see a lot more connection between my bullhorn-carrying picketers and the Pharisees than I see between them and Jesus.

Consider this:

> All this is from God, who through Christ reconciled us to himself and gave us the ministry of reconciliation; that is, in Christ God was reconciling the world to himself, not counting their trespasses against them, and entrusting to us the message of reconciliation. (2 Corinthians 5:18–19)

God reconciled the world to himself through Christ Jesus. But notice how he did this—by not counting their trespasses against them.

If God reconciles his relationship with wicked sinners by not counting their sins against them, why would we think we can reconcile sinners to God by doing the opposite? That doesn't make sense. Especially when you understand that Jesus gave us the same ministry he had—reconciliation. He has entrusted that message to us. And when all we talk about is how evil sin is and how everyone needs to stop sinning, we're not being faithful with the message God gave us.

Our message is reconciliation. How do we extend that message? By not counting people's sins against them. By extending mercy. By telling them the "good news," which is what the word *gospel* means. We tell them that God loves them and has paid for them to have perfect relationship with him for the rest of their lives.

## Just Get Jesus In

One of the best stories I have about these truths in action comes from my friend Ravi when I traveled with him in India.

The first time I met Ravi, he wouldn't let me film with him. But he did let me come along with him, telling me stories along the way. One time my crew and I went with him to a village. All the people of the village came out to meet us, and Ravi presented the gospel right away. Addressing this group that was 100 percent Hindu, he told them about Jesus.

When he finished, he simply said, "So, this is who Jesus is. Who wants Jesus?"

Everyone in the entire village raised their hand. At first, I was really impressed. But then I thought, *These guys believed in three million gods already. What's one more god to them?* They had no intention of renouncing their other gods. They simply added Jesus to the pantheon.

I asked Ravi about this later. "It seems to me that these guys are just adding Jesus to all their other gods."

He nodded. "That's exactly what they're doing."

I was shocked. "So what good does that do?"

He laughed. "Darren, our God is a jealous God. He does not like to compete with other gods. My job is simply to get him inside of people. When they get back home, they'll start praying to Jesus because he's the new god. Eventually they will realize that when they pray to Jesus, he actually answers their prayers, but when they pray to the other gods, nothing happens. I've seen this hundreds of times. Two or three weeks later, they will come to me and say, 'This Jesus is the one true God.' And they will want to have a ceremony where they burn all their other gods."

Ravi also told me stories of how people had come to him saying they'd prayed to Jesus at night and the next morning their idols were broken in half.

You know, when the Philistines received God into their temples, they thought he'd be okay sharing space with their god Dagon. They captured the ark of the covenant, the very seat of God's presence on earth, and they put it in the temple of Dagon. The next day they found the statue of Dagon bowed on its face before the ark. They set it back up, but the next morning they found Dagon's head and hands cut off and lying in the doorway, while the rest of the statue bowed before the ark (1 Samuel 5). Our God is the same today, and apparently he still treats idols the same way.

Ravi doesn't need to carry a bullhorn to tell people to repent from their pagan living. He never calls out sin. He doesn't press for people to renounce Hinduism. He doesn't run around telling people, "Hey, what you're doing is wrong. You have to stop that right this second."

## Let People Have Their Journey

Trying to force people to repent of their sins before they come to Jesus doesn't allow them to have their own journey with Jesus, where they encounter him for themselves.

God is patient, and he is jealous. He will make sure he is the only one people serve once they let him in their lives. The Holy Spirit will convict them of where they're not measuring up to his best.

Our job is simply to introduce them to Jesus. We need to be okay with simply planting a seed or watering seeds that others have sown. When I approach people on the streets, I just try to give them an encounter with Jesus. I have no idea if I'm planting a seed, watering a seed, or harvesting fruit. But when we give someone an encounter with Jesus, we have certainly done one of those three things.

If we can do that, we've done everything we are in control of. I can share Jesus with people. I can offer prayer and pray for them. I can step out, take a risk, and try to lead them into an encounter with Jesus. That's all I can do. Then I have to entrust them to God. I have to trust that God wants that person saved more than I do, that he loves them more and has more compassion on them and their eternal fate without him than I do. If I believe that, it's easy to let go of the results and trust that he will bring someone else along their path who can water the seed I planted or harvest fruit from what I watered.

Every part of the process is important, but I don't have any control over which step I get to do. I only have control over my choice to step out. If the whole body of Christ acted this way, there would be a lot of seed planting, seed watering, and fruit harvesting going on. And that's just how the body is supposed to work.

Some Christians try to strong-arm unbelievers because they want to go back to their friends and say, "We led someone to Jesus right on the spot." We don't want to say, "Well, I talked to this girl about Jesus, but she didn't want to receive him."

Those folks see themselves as independent, not part of a body that's working together to bring in the harvest. They think it's up to them, so they try to force all the steps of the journey to happen all at once. They don't trust God to continue working in someone's life, so they push that person into making the decision they want him or her to make.

This happens because we live in a culture where we need immediate results. We have newsletters to send out to people. We want everyone to sign on the dotted line right now because that will help us convince people to support our ministry. We need people to keep sending us money because ministry is our occupation.

Some people seem to think it is loving to warn people that they're on the path to hell. But the way we browbeat unsaved sinners shows that we don't trust God's compassion toward them, or his pursuit of them, or his provision for our lives. The result of this is often scorching the seed in someone's life instead of watering it.

## What You Don't Know

We don't know every detail about the person we're trying to reach. But if we pay attention to them, we can discover what we need to know.

When I was filming *Holy Ghost Reborn*, I took Todd White to Rome to see what God would set up for us to do there. The first thing we did after we arrived was take the subway to see the Coliseum. Just to be tourists. But of course, God had other plans.

As soon as we got off the subway, we saw thousands of students marching down the street to protest against the government. I felt we were in the wrong place, but Todd jumped right into the middle of the angry Roman mob so he could release the peace of God.

Todd was only in the crowd for a few seconds, with my crew and me trailing him as best we could, when he found a young man in dreadlocks. Because Todd also has dreads, the conversation started there. Todd found out his name was Enrico, then he told him how much Jesus loved him. After that first solid encounter, Todd moved on through the mob. He talked to several people who had left their faith because religion had disappointed and hurt them. Seeing people who claimed to walk with God but didn't walk like him had poisoned their faith.

Now, a month before I went to Rome, I'd interviewed singer-songwriter Kim Walker-Smith. She told me that the night before our interview she had a dream in which the two of us traveled to Rome and went underground through tunnels, and a lion walked near us to keep us safe.

At that time, I had thought about possibly filming in the catacombs of Rome, the only place I could think of that was underground, but the difficulties of doing that were pretty significant, so I gave up the idea. Until Todd came to me later that morning saying he'd had a dream, and it was essentially the same dream Kim had had. (I hadn't told him about Kim's dream.) The only significant difference between the two dreams was that Todd's included a guy in dreadlocks. God clearly had a plan for us somewhere underneath Rome, so we took the subway to get to the bus station. As we turned a corner toward the station, we met Enrico, our Rastafarian friend from the student mob.

If ever there was a God setup that was sure to lead someone to salvation, I figured it was this. I mean, there was no way for this man to explain how this crew of Americans found him, singled him out from a crowd of thousands of students, and then the next day ran into him in a different part of the city. He had to see that God had personally chased him down to show him his love.

Todd told him, "Hey, man, Jesus is real. And he wants to give you peace and a relationship with him." But he didn't receive Jesus that day. He wasn't ready.

I walked away thinking, *Well, that was weird.* It seemed like the Holy Spirit had set it all up so perfectly, but it didn't come to the conclusion I expected. Enrico coming to Jesus would've been the perfect end of the story.

The thing is, we're dealing with real lives that are complicated with emotions, histories, and all sorts of things we can't even imagine. Enrico had been hurt by the church, and that tainted his view of God. He had probably been hurt by Christians several times, and this might have been the first time anyone had told him that God isn't about church or religion.

When we reflected on it, Todd and I were excited to have been able to sow or water the seed that day. Sure, if we had kept pushing, we might have gotten him to say a prayer, but it wouldn't have meant anything. And if we had done that to someone who was already hurt by the church, that would have reinforced the lies he believed about God. It would have shown him that, yet again, church people only cared about their own agendas. They didn't care if they hurt people as long as they got what they wanted.

We needed to be okay with essentially telling Enrico, "We're going to let you continue on your journey, confident that God has you marked." And he does. I mean, God sent us into the thick of a huge Roman crowd to find this one man and gave us two supernatural dreams to guide us right to where he would be.

Only God could do that. He is the only one with that kind of targeted precision in his compassion. Only his mercy would look into an angry mob and single out a hurting heart. Only his radical pursuit would send a group of crazy Americans on a mission to show his love to one man.

That's what our God is like. He doesn't hold signs to condemn us for our sin. He doesn't shout about how evil we are. He doesn't bully us into repenting of our sin. If God doesn't do those things, why should we?

Instead, look at who God is and what he does. He loves. He pursues. He has compassion. He forgives. He releases mercy to those who don't deserve it. He chases them down no matter where they are or how hard they're running away. He determines to send his love after them until it washes over them and makes them come to their senses, turning their hearts to him through kindness, not through force.

If that's how God reaches out to lost sinners, it just might be a good idea for us to do the same.

# nine

# God Is Focused

*God doesn't always answer our prayers for healing, and we don't have a good answer for why not. This uncomfortable truth keeps many Christians from praying for the sick, afraid of what might happen if God doesn't come through. God, however, remains focused on the reason we pray—not to accomplish a healing, but to demonstrate his love.*

've made five movies that show numerous people getting healed when someone prayed for them. But I didn't put into the movies all the people we prayed for who didn't get healed or where nothing happened.

Even people who make a habit of stepping out to pray for people at every opportunity still strike out sometimes. It's a mystery.

One of the most compelling stories of this mystery comes from Bethel Church in Redding, California, an epicenter of the modern healing movement. Bill Johnson, senior leader of the worldwide ministries based there, is a fifth-generation pastor, and his father was the pastor at Bethel before him. After they began seeing revival under Bill's leadership, his dad got cancer. Everyone prayed. A number of other people who had the same kind of cancer also received prayer and were healed. But Bill's father died. How do you explain that?

This is the reason many Christians are afraid to pray for people's healing. They don't want to take the risk that the person they pray for might not get healed. They think that if nothing happens, it could ruin the other person's faith, and they might say, "Well, I always knew God doesn't exist—this just proves it." So they pray for the doctors, or pray for peace in that person's life. But they don't actually pray for healing.

## Stop Trying to Protect God

In almost ten years of filming people praying for healing, and doing some of it myself, I've never once encountered anybody who, when nothing happened, said, "Well, I knew it. God doesn't love me." Instead, people say, "Wow, thank you for taking time to pray for me."

When people tell me they are afraid to pray for healing because they're afraid of how it will affect someone's faith, I say, "You know, you don't have to be God's policeman." When we refuse to pray for someone out of fear they will lose their faith if nothing happens, it's like we're trying to protect God from himself. It's like we're saying to him, "I'm not going to go for it because you might not do anything. So instead of putting you in that position where you're a failure to somebody, I'm just going to pull back and play it safe."

God can take care of himself. We just need to trust him to be big enough to handle our situations, no matter what they are.

When fear feels real, the lie behind it sounds true. But as soon as you expose the lie to the light, you see how ridiculous it is.

The lie behind this fear is that God can't protect himself or that he doesn't care about showing his love to people. But come on. How could we possibly care about God's place in someone's life more than he does? How could we want to show his love more than he does? Jesus emptied himself of everything that made him like God, became a man, suffered, and died to show us his love, to make the way possible for us to be with him. That is his greatest pursuit of any of us, and it's far greater than anything any of us could do for someone. It's certainly far greater than just stepping out in risk to pray for someone.

Then why is it that we care more about God's reputation than he does? Does he need us to manage his brand for him? Would he hire us as his image consultants? Did he ever ask us to be his marketing directors?

Obviously, God never asked us to do any of these things for him. And in my experience, a lot more people are upset at Christians for doing nothing than for trying to do something that didn't work.

## Why Not All at Once?

Another question I get asked a lot is why we sometimes need to pray more than once for a person to get completely healed.

I've filmed situations where people get prayed for and they get healed, but only a little. They tell us their pain is better, but it's not all the way gone. So we pray again. And as we keep praying, the pain goes away more and more until it finally leaves completely.

People seem to want their healing miracles to fit into a nice little box where it's all neat and scientific—testable, repeatable, always working the same way. They want miracles to be like every other convenience in their lives, like a toaster that always works the same, a TV that turns on every time they press the power button, or a car they don't have to worry about when they sit in the driver's seat. I understand that desire, and I suppose it would be nice if miracles did that for us, but they don't. Miracles display God's creativity much more often than they display his predictability.

Whether this is God's reason behind miracles working the way they do or not, the fact that each miracle is different only deepens our need to rely on God. Intimacy with him would be left behind if we could count on a predictable success rate whenever we pray. The very unpredictability of miracles is a constant reminder that we are not the ones who perform them. It's always him in us, his power doing the impossible through us.

I don't know why miracles happen the way they do. But I do know that we are in good company when we pray based on how we feel the Holy Spirit leading us. Jesus himself ministered this way.

Jesus never ministered the same way twice. Sure, there are similarities as he ministered in similar situations, but each case was different.

John 9 tells the story of Jesus healing a man who had been born blind. Jesus was walking through Jerusalem when some of the people with him pointed out a blind beggar. They asked whose sin caused him to be blind, but Jesus said sin had nothing to do with it. Instead, he said it was so God's works could be displayed through him.

Then Jesus knelt down, spat in the ground, made mud, and applied it to the beggar's eyes. He then told the man to go wash his eyes in a certain pool. When the man did as Jesus told him, he was completely healed.

Mark 8:22–26 tells a similar story. This time Jesus was in Bethsaida, and instead of walking past a blind man, some people brought a blind man to him. This man was apparently not born blind, as the language implies he'd had sight at one time. Jesus took the man by the hand and led him out of the village, where he spat directly on his eyes and laid hands on him. Jesus' first recorded words to the blind man were, "Do you see anything?" (verse 23). The man responded that he could see men, but they looked like trees walking around. Jesus laid his hands on the man again, and this time his eyes were completely restored. Jesus instructed the man to go home, not go back to the village.

I find it interesting that Jesus used his own spit to heal two blind men. Could you imagine the headlines if some well-known pastor or evangelist did the same thing today? Imagine Billy Graham spitting in someone's face! But don't worry, it's okay, because the person was healed. Maybe this is why Jesus took the man outside the village before doing what he did.

In Jesus' day, the blind and lame were considered cursed by God, and people saw their afflictions as well-deserved punishment for sin. Because of that belief, they often spat on them as a sort of perverse way of saying, "Yeah, that's right, you sinner! You deserve your blindness!"

I can imagine what it must have felt like to be that blind man in Mark 8. After having people spit on me countless times, some people I trust lead me to a man they say can heal me. He might even be the Messiah, but he is certainly a prophet—someone who speaks for God! So I let them take me. But instead of healing me right away, he leads me out of the village and then spits in my face. I'm used to that—not that it stops hurting. But this man speaks for God. I feel like God himself has just spit in my face. I must really be a horrible sinner. Apparently I deserve this blindness. And since God gave it to me as punishment, who can take it away from me and restore my sight?

But then Jesus asked him, "Do you see anything?"

Wait, what? This man must have been in the lowest place in his whole life in that moment, but Jesus pulled him out of it with one question.

Instead of looking at his curse, the man opened his eyes and realized he was beginning to see. Jesus prayed a second time, and this time the man was completely healed.

The very act that had caused so much emotional pain in his life—being spat on—became his pathway to healing. Jesus didn't just heal the blind man's eyes but his heart as well. Maybe Jesus spat on the man to restore him emotionally from his abuse and to restore him spiritually to God, so he could know he wasn't cursed after all.

God always has a reason for what he does or doesn't do. But he doesn't always tell us. Maybe we'll never know.

If Jesus needed to pray for someone twice before he was completely healed, I don't see any problem with us doing the same thing.

## It's Not about You

Why do we feel so compelled to figure all this out? Maybe our response goes deeper than our fear of how we could impact someone's faith and how they view God. Maybe what keeps us stuck is a fear of how a "failed" prayer would impact our own faith. We're afraid of some scary questions like, "God, why would you not heal this person when I prayed for him?" We're afraid of our own inadequacy.

When Todd White first got saved, he simply read the Bible and took it seriously. He said, "The Bible says that when we pray for people they're supposed to be healed, so that's what I'm going to do."

Todd kept a written record of everyone he prayed for during those first six or eight months. He prayed for close to 750 people—and not one was healed! But he kept plugging away because he held firm to what the Bible says.

Eventually he got his breakthrough. And after that, he started diving into any situation where there was a chance to pray for people. Now, most of the people he prays for get healed.

Most people would say, "Oh well, I tried it twice and it didn't work, so I obviously don't have the gift of healing." We think this has something to do with us, but it doesn't. There can be many reasons something didn't happen.

We don't know what's going on in the spiritual realm. We don't know what invisible thing may be blocking our prayer from being answered.

Daniel prayed and fasted for three weeks before an angel came with the answer to his prayers. The angel told him that a demonic principality had withheld him for three weeks (see Daniel 10). God sent the answer to Daniel's prayer right away, but there were things going on in the spiritual realm that impacted the answer from getting to Daniel.

We also don't know what's going on inside the person we're praying for. Physical symptoms can come from all sorts of places, including emotional wounds, unforgiveness, even a person's sins. One time, when Jesus was teaching, four friends interrupted the meeting by cutting a hole in the roof of the house where the crowd gathered. It got everyone's attention as these guys lowered another man, paralyzed, on his begging mat, to the ground at Jesus' feet. Jesus looked at the man and said, "Son, your sins are forgiven you" (Mark 2:5 NKJV). When the religious people in the room took offense at Jesus forgiving the man's sins, Jesus followed through with the miracle by healing the man and restoring him physically.

Why did Jesus forgive that man's sins before he healed him? That wasn't his normal pattern of ministry. It's possible that he did it to create an opportunity to teach about his authority to forgive sins. It's also possible that what ultimately held this man to his mat was not his paralyzed body but his sin. Sin often opens a door for the enemy to work destruction in our lives. It could be that this man had a deeper issue that needed to be dealt with.

I have met many people who are afflicted by any number of

issues, but the root cause is unforgiveness. Someone hurt them sometime in their past—often egregiously—but their unwillingness to forgive opened the door to physical issues. Almost every time, when these people forgive the ones who hurt them, they are immediately healed physically as well as emotionally.

When Jesus came down the Mount of Transfiguration, he found the nine disciples he'd left at the bottom trying to cast a demon out of a boy. After Jesus finished the job, his disciples asked him why they hadn't been able to do it. (Sound familiar?) Jesus answered, "This kind can come out by nothing but prayer and fasting" (Mark 9:29 NKJV). What if Jesus was trying to clue us in on something he knew about using different strategies for different problems? What if he was telling us that different kinds of miracles happen for different reasons?

I don't know why some of my prayers get answered and some don't. All I know is that God told us to pray, so we don't really have a choice. He's the one in control, and he told me to be faithful and pray for people. My job is just to step out and leave the results to him.

## Stick to the Point

To help us get past our fears, it's important to remember the point of the whole thing. Why are we praying for people in the first place? When we see that someone needs healing, why do we ask to pray for them? What moves us to take that risk? We need to know the real answer to this question, not just the Sunday school version of the answer that we can recite. We need to know it in our hearts.

Personally, I don't think the main reason we pray should necessarily be to get someone healed. I believe the reason we pray for people is that it's a way to show them the love of God.

This is the end game for our entire Christian life, because that's what Jesus told us to do—love him and love people. Praying for healing is one way we love both God and the person in front of us.

When you realize this, your motivation changes from "I want to see a miracle" to "I just want to love you and let God do whatever he wants to do."

Paul wrote to the church in Corinth to help them make this important change in motivation. He started by outlining for them certain ways the Holy Spirit reveals himself through our lives. He wrote, "To each is given the manifestation of the Spirit for the common good" (1 Corinthians 12:7). This tells us two necessary truths. First, that every spiritual gift he's about to lay out for us is a way Holy Spirit reveals himself through us; it's a part of him reaching through us to touch the people around us and show them something about him. Second, the purpose of any gift is for the common good, not just the benefit of the person who has the gift.

Paul writes about various ways the Holy Spirit manifests himself—speaking in tongues, interpretation of tongues, healing, miracles, prophecy, words of knowledge and wisdom, and more. The Corinthians had a problem when it came to these manifestations of the Spirit. They used their gifts selfishly.

Paul couldn't have been clearer in what he wrote to them, penning the famous chapter on love—1 Corinthians 13—right in the middle of his instructions about spiritual gifts. He wrote, "If I speak in the tongues of men and of angels, but have not love, I am a noisy gong or a clanging cymbal. And if I have prophetic powers, and understand all mysteries and all knowledge, and if I have all faith, so as to remove mountains, but have not love, I am nothing" (1 Corinthians 13:1–2).

While miracles and healings are wonderful, they are nothing without love. Love is always the heart of godly ministry, whether or not that ministry sees miracles happen every time it prays.

Let's put our questions aside and stop trying to figure it all out.

Understanding is a great thing, and miracles are fantastic, but neither one amounts to anything without love.

If we all pursue love instead of asking all these paralyzing questions, our lives will be more fruitful for God's glory. More lost people will become found. More broken people will become whole. And who knows? We might even see more miracles.

# ten

# God Is Loving-Kindness

*Christians in the Western world have a reputation, and it's not a good one. We are known as greedy, self-absorbed hypocrites who only care about our own agenda, scream against anything in society we don't like, and cry as though we're being persecuted when people disagree with us. That's not the life Jesus demonstrated for us. If we embrace the way Jesus lived—love without an agenda—we will find our witness more fruitful for his kingdom.*

The contrast couldn't have been more obvious. A blind Muslim woman stood in the doorway of her house in Turkey. Two ministers engaged her in conversation, telling her about Jesus and his power to heal her physically and spiritually.

There was only one problem: the ministers had a profound disagreement over how to minister to this woman. The man, a pastor who was native to this country, insisted the woman renounce Islam and receive Jesus before he would pray for her to be healed. The woman—Heidi Baker, my friend and world-changing missionary to Mozambique—insisted they should pray for the woman first, saying that her healing would be God's demonstration of love that would bring her to Jesus.

The pastor was resolute. In the end, the woman was not healed and she did not receive Jesus. The only seed planted for God's kingdom in that woman's heart was the memory of two ministers arguing at her front door because one of them withheld love until she committed to agree with him.

I watched this failed ministry opportunity play out right in front of me at the end of my time filming *Finger of God*. I have since watched it play out over and over again in a large number of the cities I have traveled to for films.

## Why So Surprised?

My experience in Turkey takes us right to the heart of a conflict we find all around us every day. The conflict between a world that is lost and a culture within Western Christianity that's offended with the world for behaving like it's lost.

This branch of Christianity protests every perceived attack against morality within our culture. They pursue a nation that honors God officially, legislates biblical principles into US law, and behaves as a godly nation should. Now, I would love for America (or any nation) to live in a predominantly godly way. I just don't think we get there by forcing people into it through laws.

Isn't that one of the major points of the Old Testament? Israel had a legislative system that was defined as "God said these are our laws," and they couldn't keep the laws God gave them. The laws didn't produce righteousness in God's people. So why would we think it would be any different in America?

Why would we want non-Christians to behave as though they are Christians, anyway? That would make them hypocrites. And people would think they're good enough because they follow all the rules, when the gospel clearly says that we all need Jesus, no matter how good we are.

The mind-set behind this culture is almost as old as our Christian faith. It goes back to a theologian named Augustine who lived in the late fourth century, when Constantine became emperor of Rome and declared that everyone had to become a Christian or face death. Augustine's theories on God's kingdom worked well with Constantine's adoption of Christianity as a national religion. Over the course of time, Augustine's theories worked together with a nationalized religion to create a belief that if you were born Roman, you were also born Christian, because your faith and your nationality were synonymous.

That's why it was so scandalous for Luther to declare that salvation comes by faith alone. It wasn't just that it struck a contrast with salvation by works.

While Christians today aren't trying to go back to a nation where people think they are Christians simply because they were born in America, it's a similar principle. They are trying to get America to legislate Christian principles to such a degree that being born in America means you'll act like a Christian. And they believe a nation filled with people who aren't Christians but who live morally will be blessed by God.

I don't think we should be shocked by unbelievers acting like unbelievers. What does shock me is when Christians proclaim their faith but then don't live it, especially when they betray their faith in the very way they witness about their faith.

## Drop the Agenda

There's nothing that drives me crazy more than people who do things in the name of love when, in reality, they aren't doing it to love someone—they're doing it to make themselves feel good about whatever they're doing.

This happens all the time, especially in the West. I think it's because we're so programmed to be results oriented, we treat people the way those picketers treated me at my movie event. I went out to them to have a conversation, but the only reason they talked with me was to get me to repent. They had their agenda, and their agenda was the only basis for their relationship with me. If I rejected their agenda, there could be no relationship, not even a handshake.

But Christians are used to dividing over issues we don't agree with each other about. We have almost five hundred years of history defined by articulating all the ways we disagree with each other. (This is called the Protestant Reformation.) We're raised within our denominational walls to watch out for deceivers who will teach us some false doctrine, and then we define false doctrine as anything that disagrees with our denomination's theological position.

Then we do what is the most logical and reasonable thing for people with that training to do. We look at the entire world through that argumentative, divisive mind-set. We line everyone up into camps of people who agree with us and people we need to convince they are wrong so that they will agree with us.

In the end, it brings us to a place where all we care about is people agreeing with us. We only care about our own agenda.

We need to come back to the biblical truth that what brings people to change is God's kindness (Romans 2:4). What causes people to rethink their lives is when they see something better. And a fighting, bickering, petty church just looking for something to disagree with only offers them what they already have.

That's why this has become such a core principle for me as I go out to do things worth filming. This is why I always say, "Hey, let's just introduce people to Jesus. If they encounter the Holy Spirit, he'll convict them of sin, so let's just let him do it." Then the pressure is off us to try to get someone to agree with us.

## Stick to Your Job

Pattaya, Thailand, is dedicated to the sex industry. The city is undergirded by human trafficking, slavery, rape, murder, and corruption, all in the name of money.

Will Hart and I went to Pattaya to take God's love to this dark place and see what would happen. As we walked the streets during the day, we found a guy who was dressed as a girl. As best we could tell, he was a transgender prostitute selling himself to other men. People in Thailand would describe him as a "ladyboy."

What would you do in that situation? Would you immediately turn around, knowing you don't belong there? Would you make a sign to protest, and tell this man and all his potential clients how evil they are and that they need to repent or they'll burn in hell? Would you have a conversation with him, encouraging him to get his act together and quit that lifestyle?

Let me tell you, you're not going to be able to pull him out of his lifestyle in one conversation. And you're never going to see him again, so this is your one shot to influence him toward Jesus and coax him away from the darkness and toward the light. What's your best chance to point him toward God?

The approaches I listed above all have one thing in common—they are oriented toward the darkness. They are either afraid of the darkness and seek to run from it, or they cry out against the darkness and how evil it is. Christians in Western society today are known for shouting, "Hey, people who are lost in darkness! Stop being dark!"

But what if we tried something different? What if we took the light with us into the dark? What if we sat down with people like that transgender prostitute and just loved them?

That's what Will and I did that day in Pattaya. As we talked to that man and ministered to him, we learned that he lived a violent life and was repeatedly abused by his clients. They cut him with knives and burned him with cigarettes. He showed us several scars all over his body. He didn't need to be convinced that he had a bad life. He was living it every day.

He had been raised in a Christian home and kept a cross around his neck to remind him of his childhood. But he had left that faith behind long ago.

As we spoke with him, he told us he felt peace for the first time in his life. When we simply loved him, without an agenda, God's presence touched him, and he experienced something he couldn't find elsewhere.

That conversation led us to a moment where we could say to him, "You know what? In this moment, you're not a male prostitute. You're God's kid. And he wants to show you how much he loves you." Then we walked away.

Some people would consider that experience a failure. "I mean, that's great that you blessed him. You made him feel good for a minute. But thirty minutes after you're done talking with him, he's going to be back sleeping with a man for money. What good did you do?"

I have no idea what good we did. All I know is that we either planted a seed or watered one. And if enough people continue to plant and water, eventually everybody is going to be harvested.

Most people aren't interested in planting or watering because they don't see the immediate result. So they try to force the fruit to come right away. They ask, "What's the point of doing something if you can't get sinners out of their lifestyles?"

That's a very narrow view of how God moves people or draws them into his heart. It's not our job to get people out of their lifestyles, because we aren't their Savior. It's not our job to force a choice on people or to try to control their actions, because we aren't their Lord. God never put us in a place to do that. He has that place in people's lives.

We are simply God's ambassadors, pleading with the world that they would be reconciled to him. We don't do that by counting people's trespasses against them (2 Corinthians 5:18–21). We do it by releasing mercy to them. We don't need to tell them how horrible their sin is. We just need to tell them that he loves them. When we can show them how much better God is than the life they're living, they will make the trade in a heartbeat.

## It's Not Always Simple

Sometimes it takes some time to convince someone that God is who he says he is, that he's as good as he really is. They're so jaded by either the pain or the pleasure that the world has heaped on them, it takes several exposures to God's goodness before they truly believe he can heal their pain or be better than anything the world offers.

I traveled to Brazil once to film with some friends who work with prostitutes. Prostitution is legal in Brazil, and while child prostitution is illegal, those laws are not enforced. So Brazil gets a lot of sex tourism—people traveling to Brazil specifically to have sex with Brazilian girls. These girls, some nine years old or younger, will sell their bodies for just a meal or a cigarette.

Think back to your life at nine years old. What games did you play? Who were your friends? What kind of home did you live in? What school did you go to? How confident were you that the next meal would be there for you when you were hungry? What was it like to sit on your father's lap or feel your mother give you a hug? While a great number of Western Christians have experienced abuse or brokenness in their homes, very few would answer those questions the way these Brazilian girls would.

These girls' friends are probably also prostitutes. They have no home. They don't know where their next meal will come from, except that they will probably need to sell their bodies to get it. They don't go to school and have little to no education. They have no father or mother to speak of, not in the sense that we think of, and those who do are often farmed out as prostitutes by their own parents. The affection they are most familiar with is violent, abusive, painful, and perverse, leaving them no one to provide healthy affection or to bond with. And likely no one they would want to bond with.

Boys there don't have it any better. One nine-year-old boy on the streets once proudly told my friend he had killed someone that day, simply because the boy had lied about him. He thought that was normal.

As life teaches these children what the world is like, and as their worldview forms during their teenage years, what lessons are they learning? As puberty comes along and changes their minds and bodies, who do they trust to guide them through each transition?

No one.

Now, try taking some agenda-driven, pseudo-gospel message to the men and women who grew up that way. Tell them to stop their lifestyle. Tell them to quit. Demand they repent and come out of the darkness. It doesn't work. It only heaps more shame on people who are already crushed under the weight of their own brokenness.

## Stick with the Process

Those friends of mine who work with prostitutes in Brazil, Nic and Rachael Billman, are a perfect example of people who take the time to let the process do its job. There is a huge need for people like them. A lot of other people work with prostitutes in Brazil, trying to help them out of their lifestyle and give them better opportunities. But the best intentions can go wrong when love is offered with strings attached.

Nic and Rachael are building relationships with these girls. The biggest problem they have comes from other churches and Christian organizations that go to the streets to minister to the prostitutes. They say, "We're going to give you food and clothes, but at the end of our time together, we want you to say this prayer to get saved."

Really, they're saying, "Look at all these nice things we did for you. Now we'd like you to give us something." It's not much different from what these girls' clients do to them, saying, "Hey, I paid you some money, so come sleep with me."

A lot of these girls have prayed the sinner's prayer fifty times or more, and each ministry that led them to that prayer probably celebrated the "fruit" they harvested and reported that "salvation" back to their supporters. But these girls just figure, "If that's what I need to do to get food, all right, I'll say your prayer. It's a lot easier than having sex with you."

Nic and Rachael realize they can't go at the situation the same way. They need to help the girls realize that they have value in the Father's eyes. They know that people can't be saved until they first realize that the Father actually loves them. These girls won't see any transformation in their lives until they believe they're loved.

The approach my friends take is to host banquets to pamper these prostitutes. They give them the best meals they've ever eaten in their lives. They dress them up and hire a professional beautician to help them feel beautiful. They give them baggies full of gifts.

At that point most Christians would say, "Now we're going to give you the gospel message." They believe they've achieved relational capital to speak into their lives. Or they feel a burden of responsibility that while they have a captive audience they need to present the gospel in order to fulfill their job.

That's not what Nic and Rachael do. They simply say, "We're doing this because the Father loves you. Have a great night." This may not get the girls to pray the prayer as often as those other ministries do, but it forges a relationship with the girls over time.

After a while the girls start to realize, *I am worth more than how my body can please a man.* That eventually leads them to ask Nic and Rachael to pray for them and to say, "I don't want to do this anymore. I want a better life."

That's when Nic and Rachael can get these girls out of prostitution by finding them jobs and plugging them into a church. The mind-sets and beliefs that led them into prostitution had to be broken, or any rescue attempt would have been temporary. They had to become free inside before any external freedom would last.

When Nic and Rachael build relationships with these girls and show them how valuable the Father says they are, the girls are convinced of the truth, and that changes their internal realities. As soon as their internal world changes, they want to change their external world, all on their own, without anyone ever telling them they should.

## Change Starts on the Inside

Those girls in Brazil are different from the average American person in many ways, but there is much that's the same. Everyone's internal world needs to change before his or her external one will. The apostle Paul teaches that very clearly. "Do not be conformed to this world, but *be transformed by the renewal of your mind*, that by testing you may discern what is the will of God, what is good and acceptable and perfect" (Romans 12:2).

Most Christians don't seem to get the first phrase, "Do not be conformed to this world." We know we're not supposed to act like the world does. But we don't understand how that's supposed to happen.

We act like we think it's all on us to be different from the world. We take on a bunch of rules about morality because we think that's what this verse is about, and then we rely on our own strength to force our way into following all those rules so that, in the end, we won't be conformed to this world.

That's not what Paul says, though. He says we become transformed by renewing our minds. The change we need can't start on the outside with a bunch of rules that govern our behavior. It has to start on the inside, with the way we think.

If this is true for the Christians Paul wrote this to, how much more is it true about non-Christians? Our lives aren't changed from the outside in, so how can the world stop being evil without a change inside them?

The common Christian argument against this is, "We know people need a change inside them. That's why we tell them they need Jesus."

Yes, people need Jesus to change their lives. But Paul wrote this to people who already had Jesus. The solution he pointed to wasn't that they needed Jesus in their lives, but that they needed to renew their minds—to change the way they thought.

This is what happens in those prostitutes' lives. They begin to change the way they think about themselves, renewing their minds to believe how valuable they really are. When their minds are sufficiently renewed to believe the truth, the truth sets them free, and they choose all on their own to quit their lifestyle.

The answer is the same for you and me. We don't believe the same truth God believes. He has a greater truth for us to believe. And when we exchange the lie we believe for his reality, our lives change.

## Let Love Do Its Job

One day I went with Doug Addison to one of the hottest clubs in Los Angeles, California: the Supperclub.

A place like that is generally looked at as off limits to Christians. But that was exactly the point. There were people there who might not get a peek at God's light unless we went into the darkness to show it to them. Our goal was to talk to people about their tattoos, letting Doug interpret their body art to give them a word from God.

God moved in people's lives as we simply loved them. Sure, there was plenty we could have judged people for, but that would have just made them angry and shut them down. But because of love, the people at the club talked about Doug's gift and recognized God had set up our encounters.

See, it turns out God hadn't lost these people; they had just lost sight of him. They were his children; they just didn't know it yet.

The next day we went to Venice Beach. Doug prayed for people, but something wasn't right. Some sort of tension clouded over people and seemed to block the love we were trying to give out. Even when we shouted out that we were making a documentary and needed people who wanted their tattoos interpreted, we got very little response.

Finally, we spotted the reason we were having so much trouble. Parked on a busy corner of the boardwalk were several people holding giant yellow signs and a guy on a bullhorn saying, "No adulterers, nor men who practice homosexuality, nor thieves, nor the greedy, nor drunkards, nor revilers, nor stealers will inherit the kingdom of God." Well, they had just described the Venice Beach crowd, and of course they knew that. That's why they were there.

These people's misguided attempt to reach people for Jesus was getting in the way of us actually reaching people for Jesus, so I went over to talk to them. The man I spoke with explained that he felt what he was doing was the best way to love the people at the beach that day. But then he said he'd been doing this ministry for thirty years and had never personally seen anyone come to Jesus through what they did. He said maybe a few people had come to Jesus through the literature they handed out, which included the gospel of John.

I had compassion for this man and his friends. When my friends and I go out on streets around the world to show God's love, we can spend thirty minutes introducing people to Jesus and their lives have completely changed.

That's not bragging on any of the people I've filmed with or on me. It's just an example of how good God is when you let him out of the religious boxes people try to keep him in. Anyone can be fruitful in a short period of time if they love instead of judge. If they release mercy instead of bringing condemnation. If they express compassion instead of conviction.

Life is more complicated than the simple answers we try to give people. If we try to give people the boiled-down "repent" message, it won't work. We need a culture of love that meets people where they're at without trying to pull them into our world so we'll be comfortable with them.

Jesus didn't come to rescue us by calling from heaven, "Hey, humans, stop acting so human!" He didn't demand that we join his world before we could stop living like ours. Instead, he jumped into our world, put on skin, and dove headlong into our messy lives. Only then did our incarnate Emmanuel save us.

We can't save people by forcing them to leave their messy lives and join ours. We need to get to know them where they are, in the garbage dump, in their life of prostitution, in their broken marriages and families, despite their addictions, overlooking their faults for the sake of love. Only then can we convince them there's a greater reality out there.

We can't do that by shouting at them how horrible their reality is. We can only do it by demonstrating how perfectly loving our God is. And by showing them love without an agenda.

# eleven

# God Is Multicultural

*People seem to think God works more in cultures that are spiritualized, and that sometimes becomes an excuse to not ask him to move in the West's non-spiritualized culture. While it does seem true that it's easier to work miracles in nations where the supernatural is normal, neither culture nor miracles are the point. God is after people's hearts, and the only thing that changes hearts is an encounter with Jesus.*

People who watch my films tell me all the time, "The miracles in your films are incredible. Why don't we see those kinds of miracles in America?"

While we need to get over our achievement-driven, results-oriented way of thinking when it comes to miracles, I want to consider something deeper. Because this question reveals a lot about the way we think about God, the world around us, and what it takes to bring them together.

## God Is After the Heart

A lot of people will tell you one of the best things you can do to develop a well-rounded perspective on life is to travel outside of your own culture. Spend time overseas. Drive to Mexico and hang out somewhere other than a resort or the beach. If you do this, you'll find how small and limited your world is compared to all there is out there.

Now, I'm not part of a missionary organization. I have no plans to go to another country and set up something that tries to change how people live there. If I go overseas, I'm typically going to visit people who are already doing really cool stuff in that country.

So my perspective isn't one that says, "This is what happens when you take God to another culture." My perspective is more just seeing God in a lot of situations with different types of people. Based on my experience, I can definitely say that God is the same in America as he is in Korea or Africa. So in one sense, culture doesn't matter, because God is the same everywhere.

At the same time, I can also say that culture does matter. Because different cultures live with different kinds of truth, and a lot of times it's easier to move in the supernatural when you're not in an industrialized country.

India is the biggest example of this. In my opinion, India is the most spiritualized country in the world. Even the government revolves around spirits. So when you work with these people, there's one less layer you have to get through than when you're working with people in the States or in the United Kingdom. In the West, people often say, "I'm not even sure God exists." But there's no question about that in India. They believe in millions of gods.

I have seen God do way more outrageous stuff overseas than I have in my own country. Does that mean God is more willing to work in places like India than in places like America? Or does it mean that God only works miraculously in places where the gospel needs his power to validate it, as some people say?

I don't think it has anything to do with culture. I think the difference is about each individual, regardless of where they live or the culture they're a part of.

Whether God moves on a person or in a place comes down to how open people are. Yes, far more people in other nations are open to God working supernaturally than in the West. But if one of his kids opens his or her heart to him, he will respond to them, regardless of their culture or what nation they live in.

Do you want God to work supernaturally in or through your life? Then open your heart to him and begin expecting him to do it. Scripture promises that when you seek you will find (Matthew 7:7). Don't let your culture become an excuse to keep you from experiencing miraculous things. God is the same all over the world. He's just looking for someone willing to find him.

## Jesus Is the Real Deal

For a long time, when highly spiritualized people said they had powerful experiences with God, I wondered how genuine it was. I had this sense that I had to be careful how I did things with those kinds of people. I wanted to introduce Jesus to them, but since they were already very spiritual, I wanted to know how to tell if their encounter with Jesus was just another spiritual encounter to them.

This issue came up when I was in Monaco with Todd White, filming *Holy Ghost*. We were at the pier watching the massive yachts in the harbor when Todd struck up a conversation with a woman. It became clear that she was into New Age stuff. Among other spiritual things, she told us she'd gone to spirit guides and had conversed with her dead mother's spirit through them.

Todd said, "Well, let me introduce you to the Holy Spirit," and he prayed for her right there. She prayed the sinner's prayer and had an encounter with Jesus.

When it was all done, I asked her, "You've had a lot of spiritual experiences before. How does this one rank?"

"I have never felt anything like that. This was more real than anything I've ever encountered, and it was different from anything I've ever experienced."

I've heard the same thing from hyper-spiritual people all over the world. Some have traveled to hotspots or festivals to find the best mediums and guides who can give them amazing encounters—like drug addicts looking for the next big high. But when they encounter Jesus for the first time, they say, "This is the real deal. This is what I've been looking for my whole life."

Jesus is the real thing. These people have been living with a counterfeit. When they encounter Jesus, they know he's the real deal.

When Philip brought the gospel to Samaria, Acts 8 tells us that God worked all sorts of signs, wonders, and miracles through him.

But there was a man named Simon, who had previously practiced magic in the city, amazing the people of Samaria. From the least to the greatest, people were saying, "This man is the power of God that is called Great" (Acts 8:9–10).

Samaria was a highly spiritualized city, and this magician had real power, not just fancy parlor tricks. He had an incredible reputation there … until Philip showed up with the real thing.

As soon as God's genuine power and presence came to Samaria, everyone, including Simon, recognized it for what it was and left their counterfeit spirituality for the authentic Holy Spirit that Philip demonstrated.

A similar thing happened when Paul went to Ephesus and ministered there. "A number of those who had practiced magic arts brought their books together and burned them in the sight of all. And they counted the value of them and found it came to fifty thousand pieces of silver" (Acts 19:19).

Fifty thousand pieces of silver is a lot of money, and they burned it all up, leaving behind the counterfeit they had invested so much in because Paul brought them an experience of Jesus Christ, the real deal.

## How Do You Respond?

Whether you're spiritual or not, when you encounter Jesus, you know he touched you. But you may not know how to respond.

In South Africa, I filmed a man named Surprise Sitle. God saved him by waking him at night with an audible voice, telling him to run from his village. He didn't know where he was going, but he later found out his village had been ambushed and destroyed that night. Since then, he has learned to speak fourteen languages, and most of those God has supernaturally given him the ability to speak.

I prayed about where my film crew should go next, and Surprise had a vision of a remote village about four hours away. It was very small and we didn't know what we would do when we got there. But when we arrived we found the village witch doctor.

This woman was old, essentially crippled, and completely blind. Surprise and a few of his friends who had come with us (including Francis, the man who had been raised from the dead) prayed for her, then invited her to dance with them. Before long, she could both walk and see, and she testified that the Holy Spirit is the true spirit of life, greater than anything she'd known in witchcraft. Though she hesitated at fully renouncing her old life because of fear, there was no question in her mind about what was real.

Now, this is quite a dramatic story. You'd think that this old woman would show some excitement about the miracles she'd just received. But she displayed almost no emotion, not even a smile.

Surprise explained that her culture had taught her that if she laughed today, she would cry tomorrow. So out of fear and superstition, she had learned to remain steady and show no emotion.

I'm not so sure that people in Western cultures are all that different. When I took Jamie and Will to Salt Lake City, almost all of the people they prayed for experienced the touch of the Holy Spirit. But none of them knew what to do with it.

Some shook their hands as if their arms had fallen asleep. Some stood there dumbfounded. Some laughed and swore. They all knew something was happening, but they had no grid for it and they didn't know how to respond. Because if you had asked them five minutes earlier whether they believed in that kind of stuff, they would have said no.

Here in the West we think we have all the answers, but other cultures often look at us and think, *What's wrong with you guys? Of course there's a spiritual world!*

I attended the Salem witch festival with Jason Westerfield, and we prayed for a group of young men there. One was a satanist; the rest were normal American kids. As Jason prayed for one of them, the Holy Spirit came on the young man so powerfully that he fell over. The look on his face showed he was confused. He had no idea what had just happened to him.

One guy from Salt Lake City had some serious flexibility issues with his wrist. When they were healed, he stood there on the sidewalk, flexing his wrist back and forth, testing it over and over.

When I took Todd to the Korn concert, we invited people to receive prayer for anything wrong in their bodies. Todd had just finished praying for a kidney and a liver to be healed when one man stepped up and asked, "What about atheists?"

"We love you, man," Todd said. Then he told his story of growing up as an atheist. This guy had broken his back two years before. He'd recently had back surgery but still had so much constant pain that his friends called him Brokeback Joe.

Todd showed him how one leg was shorter than the other and promised him, "No matter how much unbelief you have, God loves you so much he's about to grow out your leg."

Brian, Fieldy, and all this guy's friends watched as Todd prayed for his leg, and it grew so much that it was longer than the other one. Todd prayed for this atheist until everything was right in his body. All the pain in his back was completely gone.

If you're an atheist, how do you handle that? What he had just experienced destroyed everything he believed. But he couldn't deny it, because he had seen it for himself.

You'd think this atheist would receive Jesus after having had his beliefs blown up by miracles done in Jesus' name. But he wasn't interested. Todd told him, "No pressure. We're not trying to force anyone into anything. This isn't about religion; it's about Jesus." Todd understood the seed we planted that day and simply watered it with love.

## People Need to Meet Jesus

God will work miracles for anyone anywhere. No matter where a person is from or what kind of culture they live in.

And there is no cookie-cutter way to respond to miracles. Most people will be excited and thankful. But no one can tell another person, "This is how you should respond when God does miracles." People who get caught up in how someone else is responding will miss a wonderful opportunity for what God might want to do in them.

In themselves, miracles don't draw people to God. That's why I don't think God cares whether miracles ever find us.

Jesus did miracles all the time, and it didn't cause people to truly follow him. It gave him a reputation, and crowds gathered to see him, but how many of those multitudes became his disciples? How many people experienced a miracle at his hands and chose to follow him because of it? People are the same way today. They can experience a miracle from God in their own bodies and still doubt whether God exists.

What people need is an encounter with Jesus. Jesus transforms the heart. Miracles can't do that.

Sometimes Christians, especially charismatics, get caught up in trying to do miracles. But that shouldn't be the thing that drives everything we do.

Ravi, the guy I've filmed with in India who hears the audible voice of God, travels all over the country and sees God do all sorts of incredible miracles. But Ravi's father, a Christian and a preacher, doesn't believe that God does miracles.

Ravi's father was raised from the dead. Nobody was praying for him, but he felt somebody touch him and he woke up in the morgue, surrounded by dead bodies. He freaked out and started banging on the door, needing to get out. That made all the people in the morgue freak out, because none of their cadavers had ever come back to life. Yet Ravi's father still preaches that the gifts of the Spirit aren't for today.

The most amazing things can happen to people, but that doesn't mean it will change how they see God. How you view God only changes when you encounter God himself, not when you encounter his gifts. I mean, a guy can send a woman flowers and love letters all he wants, but there's no relationship unless she actually meets him.

God tells us to be transformed by renewing our minds (Romans 12:2). When we change the way we think and what we believe, that's when our lives change. But miracles can certainly help in the process.

When I filmed with Robby Dawkins and Bryan Schwartz in Thessaloniki, Greece, God healed a girl's shoulder. Immediately she said, "God is real and I want him!" But that doesn't happen for everyone.

We need to pursue Jesus. He is the answer we're looking for. When we encounter him, our hearts change. Second Corinthians 3:18 says, "We all, with unveiled face, beholding the glory of the Lord, are being transformed into the same image from one degree of glory to another." It is the moment of encounter that transforms our lives, changing us to be like Jesus.

My life wasn't changed when my aunt and uncle received the miracle of gold teeth. What has changed me is the encounters I've had with Jesus since then.

Don't limit your Christian life to simply pursuing miracles. Pursue Jesus. Encounter him. Get to know him intimately. Let him change you from the inside out. Then, no matter who you are, where you're from, or what culture surrounds you, the God who owns your heart will work through you to find the people whose hearts are open, as long as you're willing to step out and meet them.

# twelve

# God Is God

*Throughout history, mankind has never stopped trying to put God in some kind of a box that says we fully understand him. But just when people think they understand him, God will do something that destroys the box they put him in. The truth is, there is no box you can put God in. It's not that we need a bigger box, it's that we need no box. This opens our lives to let God be God. And when we couple this with a heart that says yes to God no matter what, there's no limit to what we can do.*

God is a lot bigger than anybody realizes. He's bigger than your culture. He's bigger than your faith or lack thereof. He's bigger than your sin. He's bigger than the darkness in the world, no matter how dark it is.

God will always be bigger than anything we can throw at him. You can't find a box big enough for God.

## Freedom Is the Goal

The sooner the church realizes that God can do whatever he wants to do, the sooner we'll be able to do what he's asked us to do, which is to seek and save the lost.

We need to realize that God doesn't think like an American. In fact, I don't believe he thinks like Christians within any church denomination.

People don't want to be stuck inside a box either. They want to have freedom. I think that's what God wants too. After all, Galatians 5:1 says, "For freedom Christ has set us free; stand firm therefore, and do not submit again to a yoke of slavery." Paul wrote those words to a group of Christians he led to Jesus, but after he moved on to reach other cities, other people came, claiming to be believers and telling the Galatians they had to follow all the Jewish rules. The whole point of Galatians can be summed up in this one verse, where Paul told them not to submit to the rules again but to embrace the freedom they had in Christ Jesus.

Paul made the same point to a different audience in 2 Corinthians 3:17. "Now the Lord is the Spirit, and where the Spirit of the Lord is, there is freedom." Paul used this whole chapter to compare Moses' laws—which he called the ministry of death and condemnation—to the freedom and life we have in Jesus. He said we can't follow both the laws of Moses and the life of Jesus.

I think it's strange that so many Christians are trying to get the world to fit into these little boxes of morality, as if everything would be right with the world if we could just get everyone to follow our rules—which we think are God's rules. If rules could save people, Father God wouldn't have sent his Son to die. Rules can't save people. What we need instead is to proclaim Jesus.

## Remember Who Jesus Is

Jesus doesn't fit in any box. Any time we think we've got him figured out, he flips the script on us. He does something that challenges us, showing us another level of his goodness or grace that's more scandalous than we thought before, and then we need to start all over again.

Most boxes people try to put God in—or other people in, for that matter—have to do with all the things we have to do or can't do. The focus is on behavior rather than identity. Rules only touch behavior, but identity has to do with who you are in the core of your being.

No matter how well you know a person, you will always learn new things about them if you stay in relationship with them. Couples who have been married for sixty years still discover things they didn't know about their spouses. That's what it's like with God. As we grow in relationship with him, we continue to learn that he is way bigger and better than anything we used to know. He will always break any box we try to put him in because he is infinite.

Jesus stepped on people's toes. On purpose. I mean, one day he fed five thousand men, plus women and children, with five loaves of bread and two fish, miraculously multiplying the food. That night he walked on water to reach the other side of the lake. When the crowd saw he was gone, they pursued him. When they found him, he said to this stadium-sized crowd:

> "Truly, truly, I say to you, unless you eat the flesh of the Son of Man and drink his blood, you have no life in you. Whoever feeds on my flesh and drinks my blood has eternal life, and I will raise him up on the last day. For my flesh is true food, and my blood is true drink. Whoever feeds on my flesh and drinks my blood abides in me, and I in him. As the living Father sent me, and I live because of the Father, so whoever feeds on me, he also will live because of me." (John 6:53–57)

When the Jews around him asked, "How can this man give us his flesh to eat?" (John 6:52), Jesus said, "You do have to eat my flesh and drink my blood. If you don't, you can't have eternal life."

If a man said that to you, how would you respond? Most of us would probably leave. Which is what most of them did. Then Jesus turned to the only people still with him, his twelve disciples, and asked, "Do you want to go away as well?" (John 6:67).

Jesus never explained this, not even to his disciples. He never said, "Oh, everybody come back, you misunderstood me." He let them walk away with the misunderstanding.

Jesus also told the Pharisees they were whitewashed tombs and children of the devil. He declared over more than one city that it would be better for Sodom and Gomorrah on judgment day than for them. But he forgave the prostitute who washed his feet with her tears, and he let the woman caught in adultery go free. He spoke to the woman at the well, a Samaritan—something that was forbidden on multiple levels.

Jesus broke just about every social rule you can imagine. People tried to make him king by force, and he refused. He had every opportunity to form an army that would follow him to death, but again he refused, sending no one to death but himself. After three years of being a dominant leader for his disciples, he turned everything upside down by dressing as a servant and washing their feet.

He taught in parables that people didn't understand. In fact, he taught in parables so that they wouldn't understand (Matthew 13:10–17). The only people he explained his parables to were his core disciples. He was nothing like any pastor today. He didn't preach in clear, five-point sermons. He operated on a different level.

If Jesus was puzzling then, why wouldn't he be the same way now?

He broke every expectation people had for him. Even his

closest followers thought to the very end that Jesus was going to be their earthly Messiah who would deliver them from Roman oppression and establish Israel as the supreme nation in the world. That's why Peter pulled out a sword and began fighting in the garden of Gethsemane when Jesus was arrested. He expected war, and he was ready to die for Jesus. It's no wonder he was so disillusioned by Jesus' willful cooperation during his arrest and trial that he said, "I don't know the man!" (Matthew 26:72 NIV). He'd spent more than three years living with Jesus, yet he still had no idea of his true mission to earth.

Proverbs 25:2 says, "It is the glory of God to conceal things, but the glory of kings to search things out." God likes mysteries. The good news is, we are the ones he writes mysteries for, because it's our job (and our opportunity) to search them out. Like any good mystery, there are going to be times when we think we have it all figured out, only to come upon the next clue and have all our theories fall apart.

This life is a journey of discovery. I like knowing that I haven't discovered all there is to know about God. I like believing that I haven't figured him out and that I never completely will. While that reality is sometimes uncomfortable when I'm in the middle of mystery that I haven't gotten to the bottom of yet, it's comforting to realize how big this God is who loves me so much.

## God Takes the Long View

God always takes the long view, whereas most Christians take the short view. We want someone to change today. But behavior modification isn't a core heart change.

God will take time with you because he wants your heart and your identity to change. And that takes longer than merely making a decision to change. It's embedded in your life journey.

We frustrate people when we shout, "You have to act this way and be a better person!" Jesus simply says, "Let me in. I want to take you as you are, and for you to take me as I am. Let's be friends. Let's have a relationship. Then I can change you from the inside out. That's going to take longer than your church may be comfortable with, because they want someone who's nice and polished on the outside. But I care about your heart."

If God were in a hurry to disciple the world, he wouldn't have sent us to do it. He would have left Jesus on the planet to do the job himself. After rising from the dead, and all the miracles he did before his crucifixion and after his resurrection, I'm pretty sure he could have grown his following far more effectively than by leaving us in charge.

But God's not interested in quick change that's only skin deep. He wants real change that transforms us into his pure and spotless bride. Jesus is not coming back for a shallow, plastic-surgery trophy wife who has everything together on the outside. He's coming back for a genuine, Proverbs 31 woman, a character-to-the-core soul mate.

When I take that view into the streets as I film my friends praying for people, a person's behavior is not my first concern. People may think that means I'm soft on sin. But I'm not. I just want Jesus to convict them. It's not my job to convict them. My job is to give people an encounter with Jesus—just put him in front of them and leave them with a decision to make.

Rules are easily rejected. But Jesus is difficult to reject if you encounter him.

## Start with Your Sphere of Influence

I wonder if anyone in the church today came to Jesus through a high-pressure sales pitch. Which makes me also wonder why we don't do what did work to get us in the kingdom.

What if we went back to being authentic people who live our

lives the way God calls us to? Why can't we let go of the pressure we feel to achieve something? Let's leave behind the guilt trip we have to force someone to pray the sinner's prayer with us, and instead just be ourselves.

I learned a big lesson several years ago when I was filming *Furious Love* with Jason Westerfield. We were sitting in a hotel room in Salem, getting ready to film at the witchcraft festival. I was a little nervous because ministering came so naturally to him. He approached strangers on the street with ease, he prayed boldly without any fear, and everything he did seemed to work.

I'm an introverted guy. I don't just walk up to people. I don't go into a coffee shop or library and look for people to pray for.

I talked about it with Jason, and he said, "Not everybody is called to street ministry. But everybody is given a sphere of influence. You are called to be Jesus in your sphere of influence. And there's no getting out of it."

At that time, I was a college professor, so he told me, "Your sphere of influence right now is your students. Do you pray for your students when they're in need?"

"Yeah, that's no problem." That became the start of my stepping out in a measure of faith and risk, to begin praying with real power for my students.

What's your sphere of influence? If you're a stay-at-home mom, your sphere of influence starts with your family. Can you model what it is to be a true follower of Jesus to your children? How about to your husband? Or other family members? It doesn't have to be some big, dramatic ministry. Just show Jesus' love and take advantage of any opportunities for conversation that come up.

Do you have a job? Be Jesus wherever you work.

Jesus never told us to make converts. But if the people around you see Jesus in you, that will influence them, especially when they see how you respond to bad things going on around you. They will look to you, expecting you to judge and condemn whatever happens. And that will be your chance to show how loving and merciful God is.

## Just Be You

God didn't save you to conform you to the image of some famous evangelist. He didn't save you to conform you to the image of a world-changing missionary. He came to set you free.

If Jesus sets you free, who am I (or any other human being) to try to pressure you to do something God hasn't told you to do? Don't feel like you need to be Robby Dawkins or Todd White. You aren't them, and you weren't created to be. You are created to be exactly who you are.

That's the call to action. Be yourself—in your sphere of influence. However big or small your opportunities are, take them as they come. Love the coworker who's going through hard times, and offer to pray for him or her. Be a good employee and work hard at your job to demonstrate a positive witness to your boss and your company.

Be yourself—and simply live the gospel however that looks in your life. If every Christian actually engaged the people in their spheres of influence, the world would change overnight.

Engage with this God who is infinitely good. Take your own journey with God to find out how you can help show the world how good he is. Be set free from the rules you thought you needed to follow. Be captivated by God's love and strengthened by his bigness to try things you never have before. Work with him to discover what direction to take for your life.

I stumbled into my direction. I wasn't looking for it. God ambushed me. What's your story? And what will your story be?

# TAKE YOUR FIRST STEP

Are you willing to say yes to whatever God asks you to do? God always starts small. When God called Abraham, he didn't tell him right off the bat, "Go sacrifice your son to show how much you love me." No, the first thing God said to Abraham was, "Move. Pick up your stuff and go to a place I will show you."

The first thing God said to Moses wasn't, "Go save my people." It was, "Throw your staff on the ground."

Now, Moses could have said, "I won't do that. It's stupid." But he threw his staff on the ground. And it became a snake. Then God told him to pick it up, and it turned into a staff again.

God started Abraham out with one simple word: *move*. But how many of us get stuck at *move*? Or "Go pray for that person"? We don't say yes to God's smallest and simplest instructions, and yet we expect him to use us for big things, or we wonder why we don't see big things happening in our lives.

We will never do anything, see anything, or accomplish anything for the Lord if we just sit around, afraid to do anything.

God is looking for people who are willing to say, "If you ask me to do something, I'll do it." Those are the people who will change the world.

Will you let God out of any box you have him in? Will you let him be bigger than people's sin and your own shortcomings, big enough to handle all the cultural issues around you? Will you take up God's love as the agenda of your life? Will you let his freedom release you to serve him by just being yourself? Will you say yes to him and trust his bigness to take care of you wherever he leads you?

All he's waiting for is your yes. He can take it from there.

# ACKNOWLEDGMENTS

I've always had a love/hate relationship with book thank yous because they always seem tacked on and sort of hollow, as if you have to do this thing because it's the right thing to do—like a president kissing babies or acting like you're enjoying yourself when forced to introduce yourself to strangers at church. But in this case, not only are my thank yous sincere—they are very much needed.

I want to thank the amazing team at BroadStreet Publishing Group who painstakingly made this book possible, and who put up with my busy schedule, blown deadlines, and missed emails to still create a great book. You guys are awesome, and I think there may be some special presents waiting for you in heaven for your perseverance with this one.

I also want to thank my amazing wife, who continues to astound me with her ability to be a great mother and a great wife, as well as an extraordinary human being. Jenell, you teach me every day what it means to truly love people, and your example shows me how very far I still have to go!

Finally, I want to thank every single person who has ever filmed with me. Thank you for trusting your ministry and your heart to me, for putting up with long flights, late dinners, and unanswered questions. I am eternally grateful for friends like you, and nothing challenges me more than how you tirelessly go after God's kingdom, especially when the cameras are turned off and nobody is watching.

Jesus, this book, like everything I create, is for your glory and your kingdom. May you be made famous throughout the earth, and may your light shine in the darkness and your goodness lead all to repentance.

# ABOUT THE AUTHOR

Darren Wilson is the CEO and founder of WP Films, a film/ television production company that focuses on creating media that creatively and powerfully advances the kingdom of God. Millions of viewers worldwide have seen Darren's films. Devon Franklin, VP of Production at Columbia Pictures, calls Darren "one of the most innovative filmmakers and authors of faith today." Darren was recently named one of the "21 Emerging Leaders of Tomorrow's Church" by *Charisma* magazine.

Darren has also written two other books: *Filming God* and *Finding God in the Bible*. Both detail his spiritual journey.

Darren lives with his wife, Jenell, and their three children in Greenville, South Carolina. Connect with Darren at wpfilm.com.